Visual
Merchandising

VISUAL MERCHANDISING
PLANNING AND TECHNIQUES
SECOND EDITION

HARLAND E. SAMSON
Professor, Marketing and
Distributive Education
University of Wisconsin-Madison

WAYNE G. LITTLE
Professor, College of Business
St. Cloud State University—St. Cloud, Minnesota

Published by

D21 **SOUTH-WESTERN PUBLISHING CO.**

CINCINNATI   WEST CHICAGO, IL   DALLAS   PELHAM MANOR, NY   PALO ALTO, CA

Photo Credits

For permission to reproduce the photographs on the pages indicated, acknowledgment is made to the following:

p. 4 (bottom left): E. T. Cranston, Inc.
p. 17 (left): Hindsgaul USA, Inc.
p. 42 (upper right): Custom Interior Designs, Inc.
p. 42 (lower right): Westinghouse Electric Corporation
p. 45 (upper left): Custom Interior Designs, Inc.
p. 45 (lower left): Westinghouse Electric Corporation
p. 62: Photo Courtesy of INTERCO, Inc.
p. 73 (right): The Ford Foundation

ISBN: 0-538-04210-9

Library of Congress Catalog Card Number: 84-71040

1 2 3 4 5 6 M 0 9 8 7 6 5

Printed in the United States of America

PREFACE

In the context of this book the term visual merchandising is used to designate those efforts intended to make a business establishment attractive and effective in its merchandise presentations. The purpose of visual merchandising is to sell the image, the goods, and the services of the business. The focus of this book is on the components of visual merchandising necessary for effective presentations to customers.

The principles and techniques presented here are common to visual presentations in numerous types of retail businesses as well as in display advertising and exhibits. The emphasis in this book is on the "why" and the "how" of effective display creation.

An underlying premise is that the basic concepts, techniques, and planning procedures for visual merchandising are common to wide range of consumer goods and service merchandising. We feel that visual presentations and display can be used to (1) promote specific merchandise or services, and (2) create an image of the business. The text material and the projects are presented from the viewpoint of a worker in visual merchandising who is responsible for preparing the very best displays or exhibits possible under the usual working conditions of an operating business.

COMPETENCY BASED

The text and projects of VISUAL MERCHANDISING: PLANNING AND TECHNIQUES are based on those competencies important to visual merchandising and display work. Each text section is introduced by a listing of the learning outcomes expected through the successful completion of the section and related projects. These 56 learning outcomes cover the basic competencies necessary for planning and creating effective displays and exhibits.

ORGANIZATION

VISUAL MERCHANDISING: PLANNING AND TECHNIQUES is organized into eight sections. Each section develops a body of information important to the potential worker in visual merchandising. Section 1 describes the role of visual merchandising and the use of display in promotion and selling. Section 2 introduces the elements of visual merchandising design and the basic display principles. Section 3 explains the various types of window presentations, their use, their major components, and techniques of installation. Section 4 deals with interior display presentations, types of display units, and the location of interior displays. Section 5 covers point-of-purchase presentations and the various forms of point-of-

purchase displays. Section 6 describes the planning and construction of advertising displays and exhibits. Section 7 shows how display planning, display sketching, and display budgeting can help assure high-quality visual presentations. Section 8 discusses the various materials and tools used in the construction of visual presentations. Forty-two projects, providing for a wide range of learner interests and abilities, are correlated with the eight sections of text material. Throughout the book, there is extensive use of illustrative material that adds to the descriptions and explanations of the various topics.

STUDY SUGGESTIONS

The text material is presented as if the reader-learner is now or soon will be employed as a visual merchandising worker. The examples used are practical and realistic and are drawn heavily from those applications common to consumer goods or service businesses. Sections 1 and 2 should be studied very carefully before other sections are taken up. The understanding of visual merchandising concepts and of the elements and principles of display will provide a foundation for comprehending each of the remaining sections. Sections 3, 4, 5, and 6 provide the specifics of visual presentation in relation to windows, interiors, point-of-sale locations, and exhibits. These sections may be completed in whatever order would be most appropriate for a learner. For those learners more interested in the planning of displays and visual merchandising efforts, Section 7 may be taken up after Section 2. If the learner's interest is in the area of display construction, Section 8 may be taken up before the material in Sections 3, 4, 5, and 6.

All projects in a section, including any that are not assigned, should be read carefully before work begins on any one of them. The introductory material on many projects expands or reinforces the related text material. Instructors are urged to use supplemental learning activities suited to their community and objectives.

The authors gratefully acknowledge the photos, illustrations, and resource materials made available by numerous business firms and organizations. Particular appreciation is extended to the many teachers of visual merchandising who provided helpful suggestions on both content and learning activities. Their experiences have aided in the development of this edition of VISUAL MERCHANDISING: PLANNING AND TECHNIQUES

Harland E. Samson

Wayne G. Little

CONTENTS

1. THE ROLE OF VISUAL MERCHANDISING

The purpose of this section and related projects is to help students:

- Describe the purpose of visual merchandising.
- Explain the relationship of visual merchandising to display and sales promotion.
- Identify the major components of promotion.
- Describe how displays contribute to selling goods and services.
- Explain what customers expect of merchandise displays.
- List competencies needed by a good display worker.
- List five common jobs in display work.

The ultimate test of a store's merchandise presentations is whether they sell the goods or services offered. Successful merchandising requires offering the right merchandise at the appropriate time and at a competitive price. The manner in which a business tries to present itself to the public says a great deal about how the firm intends to attract and serve customers. The term *visual merchandising* covers those efforts intended to make a business establishment attractive and effective in its merchandise presentations. The purpose of visual merchandising is to sell the image, the goods, and the services of the store. Components of visual merchandising include building design, store layout, lights, signs, fixtures, displays, and general store decoration.

VISUAL MERCHANDISING AND SALES PROMOTION

Visual merchandising involves the presentation of a store and its merchandise in such a manner that the goods and services offered will be purchased by customers. To be effective, visual merchandising efforts must be closely coordinated with the various means of sales promotion. *Promotion* covers all seller-initiated efforts to communicate with potential customers. *Seller-initiated* means that the business firm deliberately tries to get a message to those persons who might buy the product[1] being offered.

Potential buyers include all persons, businesses, or agencies that might have an interest, either now or in the future, in buying the seller's products. Display is one form of seller-initiated effort included in promotion, and it is an activity directly related to the concept of visual merchandising. Other promotional activities are advertising, publicity, and personal selling.

Display

Display most often is defined as any form of nonpersonal presentation of an actual product to potential buyers. Simply put, display is the exposure of merchandise so that customers may see it, perhaps touch it, and select it for purchase if they desire. Display is a visual tool used by business to achieve two objectives: (1) to promote specific merchandise, and (2) to establish an image or create customer acceptance of the business. These two objectives often are stated as promotional or institutional objectives.

---

[1]The term *product* refers to anything a seller makes available at a price to potential buyers. Therefore the term covers three major categories: goods or merchandise, services, or ideas. The primary reference in this book is to tangible merchandise or goods, with special reference to services and ideas.

Displays are made up of various parts, such as background, fixtures, merchandise, floor coverings, lights, and show cards. These ingredients are arranged according to certain principles to produce displays that present viewers with a coherent visual impression. Display provides the customer with a convenient opportunity to see the merchandise and to make judgments about the use of the goods. Through its displays, a business firm can present to the customer an assortment of merchandise illustrating what the firm has to offer. Display builds on human curiosity about new and useful items. Display is an essential ingredient in most business success. It is used in hundreds of ways by businesses every day.

Advertising

Advertising consists of paid messages appearing in mass media for the purpose of informing people about a product. The media commonly used in advertising are newspapers, direct mail, magazines, radio, television, specialties, and outdoor billboards and signs. Advertising tells potential customers about a product, including who has it for sale, when the business is open, and, usually, how much the product will cost. A good advertising program will stimulate customers to come to the place of business. Once the customers are there, the store's presentation of products helps move the customers to the point where buying decisions are made, or where personal selling can bring about the sale of the products. Obviously, advertising and display must be carefully coordinated with each other as well as with the firm's overall merchandising plan if the business is to accomplish its promotional objectives.

Publicity

Publicity is any nonpaid mention of a business or product by the media. Publicity occurs when a business has some event that appears to be of interest to the public, so that the media carry descriptions of the event as news stories. Information on fashion shows, new merchandise, or special promotional events sometimes is carried as news by media. Customer interest, stimulated by publicity, can be held and even increased by effective in-store visual merchandising.

Personal Selling

The presentation of merchandise or services on a face-to-face basis between store personnel and customers is called *personal selling*. In personal selling, the seller deals individually with each customer. Effective display and visual presentation of merchandise helps bring people into the business or department of the business where personal contact can be made. The salesperson can provide the assistance necessary to bring about a sale of a product offered. Personal selling and visual presentation through display are close partners in promotion.

These promotional activities are essential to inform customers of merchandise offerings and attract them to the business location. Once the customer is at the business location, the promotional efforts must continue. The visual presentation of the merchandise and the efforts of personal selling must increase the customer's interest to the point of creating a sale. Visual presentation, particularly display, is definitely a hard-working member of the business promotional team.

Illustration 1 Promotion is the coordination of personal selling, advertising, publicity, and display. Promotion assures that all of these activities work effectively toward the same goal: sales.

DISPLAY AS A COMPONENT OF VISUAL MERCHANDISING

Product displays must be planned to fit into the overall merchandising effort of the business. For example, a firm that has decided to operate with an "open look" has set a certain task for display to fulfill. The open look allows customers to see the entire store layout from the outside or the entire selling area from the inside. The store that decides to operate on a self-service basis must have fixtures and displays that encourage that objective. The business that plans for theme shops within the store, such as boutiques, fashion centers, or specialty areas, has set forth some other specific display demands.

The visual merchandising goals and the display practices of a business must be consistent. Even the most attractive displays will fail if the store layout, lighting, and sales procedures discourage customers from buying. There is no doubt that customer activity is affected by the appearance of the business place. The inside and outside appearance of the store, the merchandise selection, and the performance of store personnel may add to or detract from the customer's acceptance of the business.

Displays in windows seen by passersby must be consistent with what will be found inside. These *exterior displays* serve as an introduction—a link between the outside and the inside. *Interior displays*—those set up throughout the interior of the store—must be inviting and easily accessible. Customers should be able to stop and examine items on display without causing inconvenience to themselves or to other customers. The store interior should give the impression of being well planned and well cared for. *Point-of-purchase displays*, which are special displays at sales transaction stations or other point-of-purchase locations, must be carefully designed to fit into the overall visual merchandising plan.

SELLING THROUGH DISPLAY

The main purpose of display is to facilitate the sale of merchandise. Display is supposed to introduce and popularize new products and to familiarize customers with new styles and products designed to make life easier or more enjoyable. Display helps a business make contacts with new customers and maintain contacts with previous customers. The purpose of a specific display is to get the customer to buy the merchandise featured.

Good Display

A good display contributes to sales by performing several functions:

1. Showing goods being used in action or indicating how they might be used.
2. Stimulating the sale of additional items or accessories that the customer originally did not intend to buy.
3. Increasing the amount of each sale by moving the customer up to a better model or quality of product than the one the customer originally planned to buy.
4. Creating an atmosphere that will invite the customer to return to the business time after time.
5. Presenting merchandise in such a way that the customer may make an appropriate selection of goods even without the assistance of a salesperson.
6. Providing the customer with enough information that obstacles to decision making are removed.

Five Steps of Selling

Displays should accomplish the five steps of selling, just as advertising or personal selling should. These steps are as follows:

1. **Attract attention.** Getting the customer's attention is an important function of advertising, display, and personal selling. If this function is not adequately performed, none of the other steps are likely to occur.
2. **Arouse interest.** Merely attracting attention is not enough. The display must hold the viewer's attention long enough to develop interest in the merchandise. Something in the display must act as a focal point. Starting from this point, the viewer should move visually through the display, taking in all the selling points the display is intended to transmit.
3. **Create desire.** In the process of looking at the display, the viewer should become enthusiastic about buying the merchandise. The advantages and features of the merchandise should stand out clearly.
4. **Build confidence.** The display should transmit a feeling of reliability and prestige. The viewer should feel confident that the merchandise is dependable and of good quality.
5. **Direct action.** If the first four steps of selling have been accomplished, buying action should result. The display should aid the viewer in taking this last important step.

Illustration 2 Visual merchandising includes the design of the store, the store layout, lighting and signs, fixtures, and—most importantly—the exterior, interior, and point-of-purchase displays.

Features of a Display

- Appropriate merchandise
- Central theme or focal point
- Information about the merchandise
- Identification of the key values of the goods
- Suggestions for putting the goods to use
- Accessibility for close-range inspection

Figure 1-1 Customers expect certain features in a good display. Above are the features most customers find helpful in a display.

WHO IS RESPONSIBLE FOR VISUAL MERCHANDISING?

It often has been said that what becomes everybody's business soon becomes nobody's business. This is true when it comes to visual merchandising and the visual presentations of merchandise. Obviously top store management determines the image and type of business atmosphere that is desired. This policy-level decision then must be communicated to those who are responsible for the business planning, visual merchandising, and sales promotion.

Display certainly should be a concern to all persons in the business, but the responsibility for displays must be assigned clearly to specific workers. In larger firms, this usually is done by the appointment of a visual merchandising or display director. The director then builds a staff of display workers as needed by that firm. In some smaller businesses, the owner or manager may assign display work to persons who carry out other duties as well. Care must be exercised in making such an assignment. When display work is given to inexperienced or uninterested employees, the results often are unsatisfactory.

The display work to be done by various workers within a business should be fully described and specifically assigned. If salespeople are to be responsible for the set up and maintenance of counter displays, then this should be made clear to them. If the person doing the advertising work for the firm also is supposed to plan and carry out the display function, that, too, should be clearly understood. The well-organized business will have display responsibilities specifically assigned to individuals who are prepared and able to perform those duties.

There are five common job titles in display work. Descriptions of these positions follow:

Illustration 3 Larger businesses, with many windows and extensive interior displays, will have a full staff of display workers to plan, prepare, and install displays.

Illustration 4 Small businesses may have their displays installed by workers who also have other responsibilities. It is important that display responsibilities be assigned clearly.

1. **Visual merchandising director or manager.** The person responsible for planning and creating the visual presentations of the store often is at the same level as the person responsible for the advertising activities. The visual merchandising director is responsible for creating all exterior and interior displays, directing the work of other

display employees, and coordinating display efforts with the efforts of the advertising and merchandising directors.

2. **Display specialist.** A worker knowledgeable in all aspects of display or especially talented in one aspect of display (such as design, construction, lighting, or animation) is referred to as a display specialist.

3. **Display assistant.** Assistants usually are beginning display workers who assist the display specialist in construction, installation, and maintenance of displays. The assistant also performs general housekeeping duties in the display department.

4. **Trimmer.** A trimmer is a worker who has more experience than the assistant and is more skilled in arranging displays, selecting and using appropriate accessories, fitting mannequins, and working from designs prepared or selected by the director.

5. **Free-lance specialist.** An individual who is skilled in display work and who provides his or her services to a business for a fee is called a free-lance specialist. Free-lance specialists may be used by firms that do not have a display staff or that need special help for a particular project. In addition to being skilled in display, the free-lance specialist also must be able to make accurate estimates of the cost of materials and the time needed to do a specific display job.

PREPARING TO WORK IN VISUAL MERCHANDISING

A good beginning point for a career in visual merchandising is work in the display area. The basic training needed to enter display work is a good foundation for dealing with the broader activities included in visual merchandising. Individuals with display-related training are most likely to get a display job. They then can progress to higher-level jobs and assignments. High school courses, adult education courses, and programs offered by community colleges are good starting points. Basic courses in marketing, selling, advertising, display, art, and retailing provide a basis on which to build advanced training in visual merchandising skills. If you are dedicated to becoming a professional in the field, then you should consider a four-year college program which includes work in business as well as in the visual arts.

In planning your career in visual merchandising, you should recognize that the work varies

considerably from one business firm to another. In a small business, one person may be "the display department" and do everything. In larger firms, the display worker is a member of a team and quite likely would be expected to develop some special ability in certain types of display work. Work hours probably will be irregular in almost any display job. When displays must be installed and when seasonal work is heavy, you may put in extra time. Because displays often must be removed and installed when customers are not around, late evening, early morning, and weekend work hours are common.

Customers today are careful shoppers who have developed an awareness of quality. Increasing excellence of visual merchandising is necessary to impress customers who see many outstanding displays in shopping malls and view the multisensory presentations of merchandise on television. Visu-

---

Competencies of a Good Display Worker

- An understanding of the importance of display and of its contribution to the effective sale of merchandise.

- The attitude that good display is essential to building the image of a business and that it serves as a major means of educating customers to new styles, uses, and values of merchandise.

- The ability to create and employ effective seasonal and storewide themes for display.

- A knowledge of the principles of effective display design.

- A knowledge of the types of arrangements appropriate for interior, exterior, and point-of-purchase display spaces.

- A knowledge of and ability to use a variety of fixtures, materials, and tools for creation of displays.

- A knowledge of sign techniques and the ability to design and letter display signs.

- A knowledge of how to select and secure merchandise and accessories for a display.

- The ability to perform the tasks necessary for proper record keeping and housekeeping within a display department.

Figure 1-2 A good display worker must possess knowledge and ability in several areas and must understand that display is essential to a business.

ally exciting displays are needed, which presents a distinct challenge to persons entering display work. In spite of the sophistication of today's customers, experts indicate that the basic display concepts are still essential for eye-catching presentations that will attract customers into stores and encourage them to buy.

SUMMARY

Visual merchandising includes those efforts intended to make a business establishment attractive and effective in its merchandise presentations. Display, one of the four main components of promotion, is a fundamental visual tool used by businesses to achieve a direct, non-personal presentation of merchandise so that customers may see and handle the goods and select items for purchase. Display attempts to accomplish the five steps of selling — attract attention, arouse interest, create desire, build confidence, and direct action. Display jobs range from management level to the entry or beginning level. Training in marketing and visual merchandising plus experience in display work are essential for movement to higher-level jobs.

2. VISUAL PRESENTATION CONCEPTS

The purpose of this section and related projects is to help students:

- Identify specific goals that display personnel may have in mind when planning and constructing visual presentations.
- List and describe the various elements of a visual merchandising design.
- Select color combinations that will create a pleasing and attention-getting effect.

- Describe the principles of visual merchandising design and explain how these principles can be used with display elements to create effective visual effects.
- Recognize the basic visual merchandising arrangements commonly used to present merchandise.
- Select display arrangements appropriate for different types of merchandise.
- Explain how the techniques of depth and motion can improve the effectiveness of a visual presentation.

Visual presentations of merchandise that bring forth comments of "Beautiful," "Stunning," "Exciting," "Dynamic," or "Superb" usually are based on a sound foundation of display fundamentals. Putting together a presentation (display) that will accomplish the designer's goal requires a good understanding of several fundamental concepts regarding display elements, principles, color, and arrangement. When you understand these concepts, you will be able to produce displays that will draw "rave reviews."

GOALS OF VISUAL PRESENTATIONS

Creators of visual presentations have specific goals in mind when planning and constructing their arrangements. These goals include: (1) creating visual presentations that will sell merchandise, and (2) presenting a favorable image of the business to the buying public. Remember, however, that there is more to creating a good display or exhibit than simply placing merchandise in a neat pile where it can be seen by the customer. In fact, some business people are convinced that an art background is absolutely necessary for display work. Others feel that display design is some sort of mysterious art form. You can be sure, however, that this is not the case.

TECHNIQUES FOR EFFECTIVE DISPLAYS

Leaders in the visual merchandising profession generally agree that a set of basic display elements and principles does exist. Mastery of these basics can help an individual acquire a feeling for what is pleasing and what is not. With study and practice, the beginner gradually will acquire the skills needed to design and construct effective displays. Effective displays will sell merchandise and create a favorable impression.

In order to use the various elements and principles of visual merchandising, it is important that you be able to recognize clearly the difference between the two. An easy way to understand this difference is to remember that *elements* deal with the appearance, or *features*, of what is being displayed. (This can include the display area as well as the merchandise.) *Principles* deal with the thoughtful *placement* of the elements in the display. Just remember this easy formula: elements (features) + principles (placement) = display design. (Various types of standard merchandise arrangements will be discussed later.)

When visual merchandising elements and principles are combined properly, the result is a visual presentation that creates the desired mood or impression. Remember, however, choosing merchandise that is competitively priced and timely also helps make displays effective.

ELEMENTS OF VISUAL MERCHANDISING DESIGN

Display design elements include line, shape, size, weight, texture, and color. Each element is a part of the physical appearance of the products being displayed. These elements can have a strong influence on the impressions customers receive when they view the display. Examples of these influences will be presented as each element is reviewed.

Line

The element of *line* comes from the physical outlines of the merchandise items being displayed and from their placement. Lines in a display can control the direction a customer's eyes will travel while viewing that display. Lines also can create certain moods or impressions. For example, straight lines can create an impression of rigidity, stiffness, or control. Curved lines, on the other hand, tend to communicate a feeling of flowing movement or freedom. The angle of a line is also a means of communicating mood or feeling. Vertical lines establish a feeling of height, dignity, poise, or dependability. Diagonal lines indicate action or movement. Horizontal lines can give a feeling of width or of quiet, calm, or confidence.

Impressions made by lines, when they are organized according to design principles, help to establish the feelings desired by the display person. Above all, an effective job of leading the customer's vision from one item to another can be accomplished.

Shape

Lines arranged in certain combinations can produce a variety of shapes. *Shape*, as an element in display designing, serves as one means of describing the physical appearance of merchandise. But the element of shape is by no means limited to the merchandise itself. It is also an important factor in describing *display units* and deciding how these units can be used to best advantage. Shapes such as squares, cubes, rectangles, circles, ovals, and triangles are typical of the forms that display units or areas may take. These shape names indicate something about the height, width, and sometimes depth of a specific display area. It is possible, however, to work with display units that have no distinct shape.

Units of this type are referred to as *open* or *mass displays*. Such display units have a floor (usually the floor of the store), but no sides, background, or ceiling. Regardless of whether the area is open or enclosed, shape deserves consideration when you are selecting the display unit and the merchandise to be displayed.

Size

Size is perhaps best understood when discussed in terms of relationships between things. Most people tend to describe size by comparison. They say, "It is taller than you are," or, "Their new car has more storage space than a truck." In display work, size describes the relationship between the merchandise and the display space available for that merchandise.

As another element in display design, size plays a major role in limiting what the display person can or cannot display. It would be unsuitable, for instance, to place large items such as dresses or suits on mannequins in a unit designed to display blouses, shirts, shoes, or accessories. The size of the objects used relates directly to the principle of proportion, which will be discussed later.

Weight

Perhaps the easiest way to determine the physical weight of something would be to place it on a scale. As an element of display design, however, *weight* refers not only to actual weight but to the impression of weight created by the appearance of the display item. Have you ever tried to guess the weight of something before picking it up or weighing it? You may have found that the item was heavier or lighter than you thought. This happens because our judgment of weight is based either on our past experiences or on the appearance of the item.

The larger the product displayed, the more likely that it will be judged heavier than items of smaller size. Also, the darker the color, the heavier the product will appear. Besides size and color, the line, shape, and texture of the product can influence the appearance of weight.

The element of weight can prove valuable to the display person who knows how to use it correctly. The two major uses of weight in display work are (1) to direct the vision of the potential customer, and (2) to bring attention to the most important items in the display. These uses will be discussed later in the discussion of balance as a principle of design.

Diagonal

Curved

Vertical

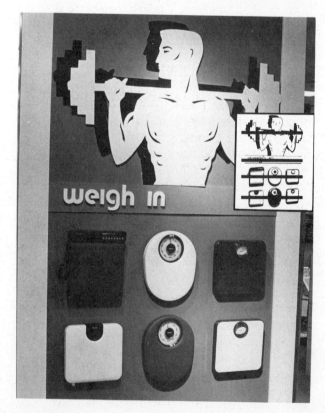

Horizontal

Illustration 5   A choice of line may establish the mood and impact of a display.

Illustration 6   Triangular display unit.

Illustration 7   Round display unit.

Illustration 8   Rectangular display unit.

Illustration 9   A very large display presentation is a challenge to the display designer. Can you see how the elements of size and weight have been presented successfully here, primarily through the use of appropriate accessories?

Texture

Texture refers to how a surface looks or feels. When we say that a product looks shiny or dull or that it feels smooth or rough, we are describing its texture. In display work, texture can be real or it can be created.

Let us say that your employer has asked you to build a display featuring stainless steel cookware. The display unit to be used has a smooth, shiny texture similar to that of the cookware. There is no contrast between the display unit and the cookware. Since a goal of display is to draw attention to and sell merchandise, something needs to be done. To create contrast, an impression of rough background texture could be created by shining a floodlight through a piece of screen located behind the cookware onto the display background. This would show up as a pattern of tiny squares on the display background, providing the necessary contrast in texture and attracting the eye of the customer to the shiny surfaces of the cookware.

Illustration 10 Note how the contrast between the textured background and the smooth finish of the merchandise draws attention to each product.

Color

Of all the visual merchandising elements, **color** provides one of the best ways to attract customers. Color promotions are a regular part of display in fashion merchandising. Certain colors can come into style because of their wide use in display. More clothing or more carpet may be sold just because customers want the "latest colors."

Color, properly used, can give a display that touch of "something special." However, because color is a powerful element, it must be used carefully. Color used poorly can destroy contrasts between merchandise and cover up the main point of a display. In fact, too much color can confuse and even irritate some customers.

Considering how color can affect the customer's mood while he or she is making buying decisions is important. In display, certain colors have long been linked with certain impressions on shoppers. Red means power and strength while blue, the all-around favorite, creates an impression of calm and quiet. Yellow is a happy sunshine color, while violet suggests quality and richness. "Warm" colors (red and orange) are exciting. "Cool" colors (blue and green) are calm and relaxing. As a result, it is felt that the apparent temperature of a color may affect customer demand for displayed merchandise. Some display people believe that air conditioners are best displayed using cool colors. Electric blanket or heating pad displays may sell more merchandise when warm colors are used.

Color Tips for Display

- As few colors as possible should be used in any one display.
- Color values and intensities can be used to maintain unity in your design.
- Each season may have its leading colors. Be ready with up-to-date displays.
- Colored lights shining directly on merchandise often distort and misrepresent merchandise colors. Check the effect of your lighting.
- Use of too many colors or too-bright colors may attract attention away from the merchandise.
- One color should be emphasized in a color scheme. The other colors should blend with it or serve as tasteful contrasts.

Figure 2-1 The list above contains some essential points about color that can be helpful to the beginner or the professional in designing displays.

The professional display person should be familiar with basic color terminology and should know what happens when various colors are mixed. *Hue* is just another name for color. Red, green, blue, and so forth are hues. *Value* is the lightness or darkness of a color. It is altered by adding a darker or lighter color, often black or white. The lighter values obtained by adding light colors or white are called *tints*. The greyer values created by adding darker colors or black are called *shades*. *Pure colors* (full strength) are free from added darks or lights. *Intensity* refers to the brightness or dullness of a color.

Relationships between various colors and the effects that color combinations can create are sometimes hard to understand. In order to visualize these relationships, many people use a device called a *color wheel*. The color wheel serves as a guide in selecting color combinations that will be pleasing to the eye of the customer. *Complementary colors* are found directly opposite each other on the color wheel and create the greatest contrast. A small amount of one color added to its complement can produce interesting "fashion" shades. However, when mixed in equal parts complementary colors will form drab shades. *Adjacent colors* are those located next to each other on a color wheel. They contrast with each other only slightly and provide harmony. The color wheel contains a full range of color combinations which can produce the degree of contrast or harmony desired by the display designer.

Keep in mind that color in display work is not limited just to the merchandise. The display unit, merchandise props, and area lighting also can add to or take away from the effectiveness of colors, depending on how each is used. Effective displays can be produced by: (1) using as few colors as possible, and (2) selecting colors that will provide a pleasing emphasis on the merchandise being displayed and not draw attention away from it.

PRINCIPLES OF VISUAL MERCHANDISING DESIGN

It is important to know what display *principles* are and how they can be used with the elements in display design. Earlier it was stated that *elements* deal with the appearance, or features, of merchandise being displayed. Remember that the elements are line, shape, size, texture, weight, and color. Principles of visual merchandising help the display person decide where merchandise can best be placed in a display unit.

Principles of visual merchandising include harmony, contrast, emphasis, proportion, and balance. Although each principle is discussed separately here, keep in mind that one or more of these principles can be found, together with various elements, in every good display. For that reason, examples of how principles and elements work together will be presented in the following material.

Harmony

Harmony in display is like harmony in music. When many different voices blend (sound good together), they are said to be in harmony. But a

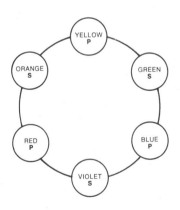

PRIMARY **(P)** AND
SECONDARY **(S)** COLORS

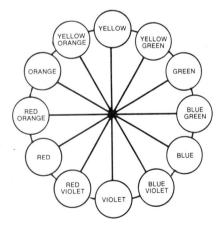

COMPLEMENTARY (OPPOSITE) COLORS

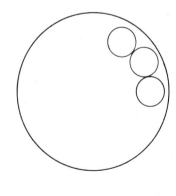

ANALOGOUS COLORS
(ADJACENT, OR SIDE BY SIDE)

Figure 2-2 Various color relationships are shown in the diagrams above. The basic 12-part "color wheel" is shown in the center.

Effect of Colored Lights on Various Colored Materials

Original Color of Item	Color of Light Falling on Item					
	Red	Orange	Yellow	Green	Blue	Violet
Black	Violet black	Deep maroon	Olive	Green brown	Blue black	Violet black
White	Red	Orange	Light yellow	Green	Blue	Violet
Red	Intense red	Red orange (Scarlet)	Orange	Brown	Blue violet	Red violet
Orange	Orange red	Intense orange	Yellow orange	Green yellow	Brown	Brown
Yellow	Orange	Yellow orange	Yellow	Yellow green	Green	Brown (reddish)
Light green	Gray (reddish)	Yellow green	Green yellow	Intense green	Blue	Light brown green
Deep green	Black (reddish)	Rusty green	Yellow green	Intense green	Green blue	Dark brown green
Light blue	Violet	Gray (slightly orange)	Yellow green	Green blue	Bright blue	Light blue violet
Deep blue	Intense violet	Gray (slightly orange)	Green	Blue green	Intense blue	Bright blue violet
Indigo blue	Violet black	Maroon (slightly orange)	Dull green blue	Dull green	Dark blue	Deep blue violet
Violet	Red violet	Maroon (reddish)	Maroon (slightly yellow)	Brown (slightly blue-green)	Deep violet blue	Deep violet

Figure 2-3 The use of various fluorescent lights and other special types of bulbs may create unexpected effects when the lights shine on the colors of fabrics and other display materials. Find pairs of complementary colors, as shown on the color wheel. Note that complementary colors "cancel out" each other's color power when mixed. As you can see from the table above, mixing complementary colors results in a shade of brown.

sour note can ruin the entire song. Likewise, when different items of merchandise are placed so that they blend (look good together), they also are said to be in harmony. A poor blend means a poor display.

Harmony in visual merchandising results when related items of similar line, size, shape, texture, weight, or color are placed together in a display unit. Merchandise elements, like singing voices, can be different, but they must fit together if they are to harmonize.

Contrast

Contrast refers to differences seen in things being compared. Contrast among the elements of color, shape, and size of the items displayed provides an excellent way to call attention to the merchandise. But be careful. Contrast is more difficult to use than other display design principles. It has a powerful effect on the customer's visual attention. Sharp contrasts may confuse the customer. They also may cover up the real purpose of the display — to sell merchandise. For instance, placing ice skates, vacuum cleaners, and swimming suits

together in a display unit would provide contrast. However, there might be many confused customers as a result. With practice, display people are able to develop judgment in determining how contrast can be used to enhance a display rather than to detract from it.

Emphasis

The principle of *emphasis* is used in display work to direct the customer's attention to key items. The merchandise itself is often the object of emphasis. But a sign with important information about the items being displayed also could be used. One item or the other must be chosen for emphasis. It is possible that emphasis could take the form of an entire display filled with the same merchandise.

Regardless of where it is placed, the main emphasis always should be clear to the customer. Generally, emphasis should be placed on only one item. Never use more than three items or the effect will be lost. When designing a display, keep in mind that the display elements — line, size, shape, texture, weight, and color — can create the emphasis desired. Properly handled, emphasis can create a strong visual effect for the display.

Proportion

Customers want to see merchandise presentations that are pleasing to look at. Part of getting that pleasing look into a display comes from careful selection of merchandise. Select items that have shapes and sizes that fit well together. The eye expects objects it sees to have a pleasing relationship in size and shape, or **proportion** to one another. This includes the display unit as well. When various objects do not seem to belong together or do not fit properly in the space provided, they are said to be "out of proportion."

For instance, the combination of diamond rings with lawn mowers in a large window display unit probably would not be pleasing to the eye. The differences in the sizes and shapes of the merchandise would be too great. The display area would be too large to create any effect for the rings. Large objects crowded into a small display unit also would look out of proportion. If lawn mowers were placed in a display space normally used for jewelry, the result would be an ineffective display. Keep in mind that the chances of achieving proper proportion in designing displays will be increased greatly if you give careful consideration to the elements of size and shape in choosing merchandise and display space.

Balance

The principle of **balance** in visual merchandising design may seem a little confusing at first. Think of balance in terms of a playground seesaw. As a child, how did you try to keep the seesaw board level? Probably you got someone close to your own weight to sit on the opposite end of the board. Sometimes the board would not stay level, so that either you or your partner had to move closer to the middle to balance the difference in weight.

On the seesaw, you were dealing with actual weights to achieve balance. In display, the optical weights of merchandise, rather than their actual weights, are used to get balance. The idea, however, is the same. **Optical weight** refers to the appearance of merchandise and to the fact that some items look heavier or lighter than others. Elements such as size, shape, and color of an item can give an impression of weight to the eye. These differences in appearance make it necessary to compare the optical weights of the various items of merchandise being considered for a given display area. Like the

true weights on the playground seesaw, optical weights must be placed carefully if balance is to result. There are two types of balance in display work: formal and informal.

FORMAL BALANCE

Formal balance in design is just what the name implies. It is a stiff, formal arrangement in which every item placed in one half of the display area is offset by a similar item placed in the other half of the display. Formal displays sometimes are less interesting to look at than informal displays. But they are easier to design and can do an effective job of selling merchandise.

The first step in planning formal balance in a display is to draw an imaginary line down the center of the display area. Then, begin to place merchandise in the display space. Be careful that the optical weight of a display item on one side is not greater than that of the similar item on the opposite side. The secret to achieving a formal balanced look in display will depend on your ability to optically weigh the items that are being placed in the display area. This skill will come with practice and close observation of the merchandise you select.

INFORMAL BALANCE

Informal balance makes it possible to display merchandise in a more unusual and often more attractive way than formal balance allows. Planning informal balance also requires that you draw an imaginary line down the center of the display area. But items placed in one half of the display unit are not necessarily matched by identical or similar items in the other half. Informal balance is kept by placing items of merchandise with *different* optical weights on each side of the imaginary center of the display area and *still* balancing the two sides. For instance, it might be necessary to place three light-colored shirts on one side of a display unit in order to balance a darker colored sport coat on the other side. With practice, you will learn to optically weigh the objects to be used in a display. Eventually it will become easier to place items so that you end up with a feeling of equal weight on each side of the center point.

Informal balance lends itself to the creation of interesting and attention-getting displays. Variations in line, size, color, texture, shape, and distance from the optical center can affect optical weight and make it possible to visually balance informal displays. When well done, informal balance will give displays more style and appeal than formal balance will.

Contrast

Proportion

Emphasis

Harmony

Illustration 11 Four of the principles of visual merchandising design are shown in these displays.

Illustration 12   Balance, the fifth principle of display design, can be expressed formally or informally. Note how both the formally balanced arrangement on the left and the informally balanced arrangement on the right serve to draw attention to related merchandise as well as to the major items.

BASIC VISUAL MERCHANDISING ARRANGEMENTS

It may be helpful to know that there are five basic display arrangements to which you can refer in developing your own display design skills. Although a number of names are used to describe these arrangements, they generally are called repetition, step, zigzag, pyramid, and radiation. A brief review of these basic arrangements, with examples of each, follows.

Repetition

Repetition refers to a repeated design. In display work, arrangements using repetition can be built quickly simply by placing one kind of merchandise in rows stacked on top of each other until the desired display size is reached. Spacing and direction of the merchandise are repeated over and over in the display unit. Because arrangements by repetition can be dull to look at, their greatest use is with highly advertised consumer products such as those found in food, hardware, and discount stores. Retailers who use large displays and self-service to sell merchandise find repetitive arrangements well suited to their volume operations. Repetition works for these merchants because they depend on well-known merchandise to attract customer attention.

The location of displays using repetition is also an important consideration. Placing these displays in heavy customer-traffic areas (near checkout counters and at the ends of merchandise aisles) can increase their effectiveness.

Step

Step arrangement provides an opportunity to place merchandise in straight lines at different heights or levels in the display unit. Often the steps are equal, so that the display design is very much like steps in a real staircase. Shoes often are displayed in this manner. Step arrangement is a little less formal than repetition. It also does a better job

Illustration 13 Repetition can create an effective display design.

Illustration 14 This front-view step arrangement dramatizes small objects through the use of pedestals.

of controlling the customer's line of vision. As a general rule, three steps in a display are usually enough unless the items are small.

Step displays may be designed with the lowest step in the front and the highest in the back. Step arrangements also may be presented using a side view. Only the display designer's imagination limits what can be used to create the actual steps on which the merchandise is placed. Platforms, stands, shelves, bricks, boxes, even different sizes of the merchandise itself, provide effective and interesting steps. If you are looking for a display design that requires little merchandise, appears to fill space, and highlights specific items, step arrangement can be a good choice.

Zigzag

Zigzag arrangement is really a variation of the step design just discussed. As the name implies, merchandise is placed in a pattern following a zigzag line. Zigzag does not require equal height and distance between each level of merchandise. This unevenness results in a more informal balance.

Zigzag, like step arrangement, sometimes may consist of several levels, with the highest level placed at the rear of the display. The display designer must be careful, however, not to allow too much distance or height between each of the merchandise levels. If this happens, the merchandise will not tie together visually and the zigzag effect will be lost. Properly placed, zigzag arrangements result in interesting and attractive displays that sell merchandise.

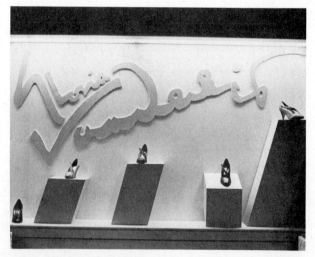

Illustration 15 Merchandise arranged in a zigzag fashion can lead the viewer's vision from one product to another.

Illustration 16 Various visual merchandising arrangements can be combined effectively. Here step, zigzag, and repetition are used.

Pyramid

A *pyramid* arrangement is built in the form of a triangle standing on its base. It consists of several straight or curved rows of merchandise narrowing upward to a peak. This basic arrangement is easy to construct and is very effective when used to display canned goods or hard-covered packages.

Pyramid arrangements usually are examples of formal balance. They can be stiff and uninteresting to look at. When combined with other merchandise arrangements, however, pyramid designs provide a way of bringing the customer's attention to specific items in the display. For example, let us say that you are employed in the display department of a discount department store. Your store manager has asked you to build a large display of hair dryers that are on sale. It is decided to use repetition arrangement to do the job. Unfortunately, the sign that must be used with the merchandise is too small for the size of the display being planned. One solution would be to add a pyramid of hair dryers at the base of the display, with the sign placed in the center of the pyramid. This combination of repetition and pyramid arrangements would make it possible to build a large display. At the same time it would direct the customer's attention to the sign located in the pyramid of hair dryers.

Radiation

Display designers use a variety of examples to describe what *radiation* arrangement in display means. A radiation arrangement can be compared to a wheel with spokes, a starburst, or rays around the sun. Notice that each of these examples contains both a center and lines which go out (or radiate) from that center.

As an example, assume that a shipment of sweaters has just arrived in time for a special promotion. Keeping in mind the comparison to a spoked wheel, consider how a radiation arrangement could be used to display the sweaters. With the most important style of sweater in the center of the display unit, other sweaters could be placed in straight lines going out from the center. The effect would be to draw the customer's eye to the sweater in the center of the display. Or a single sweater could be placed in the center of the display unit and radiating lines of scarves could be arranged to draw the customer's attention to the sweater.

Radiation can be used with many types of merchandise display. If the goal of the display plan is to attract the customer's attention quickly to a certain item, a radiation arrangement can do this very effectively.

Illustration 17 Radiation arrangements can be effective in drawing attention to single-item displays.

DEPTH AND MOTION IN VISUAL PRESENTATIONS

When you plan display designs according to the various arrangements mentioned here, you will realize that sometimes these arrangements may be flat, like pictures. But sometimes they will have **depth** as well as height and width. This means that merchandise may be placed at varying distances

Illustration 18 Use of depth in a display can draw attention to merchandise contrasts.

from the front, back, top, bottom, or sides of the display unit, as long as the principles of display design are kept in mind. At another time, a fixture may be used that will revolve the display. This **motion** will allow all sides to be seen by customers. The motion itself usually attracts attention. (See Section 8 for information on motion and animated devices.)

When an extra effect that comes from depth or motion is included in a display design, the finished arrangement may attract great customer interest. With this attention from shoppers, sales of the displayed merchandise can develop more rapidly.

SUMMARY

Most successful display designers apply several concepts and skills in their daily work. Display designers understand and make use of various elements and principles of visual merchandising. From the descriptions and examples provided in this Section, you should understand the popular display arrangements currently in use in the display industry. The value of depth and motion techniques as a means of creating special display effects also may be familiar to you from your experience as a customer.

Visual merchandising can indeed be an exciting, creative, and dynamic field. And it need not be a complicated one! Those who are willing to take the time necessary to learn what it takes to create effective visual presentations will find that this work is satisfying in itself and also can be a basis for job advancement.

3.   WINDOW PRESENTATIONS

The purpose of this section and related projects is to help students:

- Describe the value of good window displays.
- Identify the various types of window display units.
- Describe the purposes of various types of window displays.
- Identify the components of a window display.
- Select merchandise appropriate for a window display.
- Build an effective window display.
- Understand the procedures necessary for an efficient window display installation.

Whether they occur along a street or in a shopping mall, exterior windows offer a store a major means of visually presenting merchandise to customers. Often merchandise presented in a window display will cause a passerby to stop, come into the store to examine the goods, and perhaps buy. For many customers the first visual impression of the store and its merchandise comes from what is presented in a window display. A carefully crafted arrangement of mannequins dressed in the latest fashions or of merchandise items on attractive fixtures under special lighting can create a visual impact difficult for customers to ignore.

VALUE TO THE RETAILER

Good window displays can be of tremendous help to the retailer in selling merchandise. Even though most window displays are seen by passersby for just a few seconds, certain positive actions can result. First of all, the shopper's attention may be captured. Second, the potential customer may enter the store seeking additional information about merchandise displayed. Third, and better yet, the customer may buy a displayed product even without additional help. In this case the window display has sold the merchandise, and that is really what display is all about. Fourth, window displays that draw people into a store can give the retailer an opportunity to "put the best foot forward" in getting and keeping new customers.

Techniques used to develop effective visual presentations in store windows vary widely. The purpose of all such presentations, however, is the same — to sell merchandise and to create a favorable image for the retailer or business. The information in this section should be helpful to you in planning and constructing visual merchandise presentations for store windows.

TYPES OF WINDOWS

From the standpoint of store or building design there are three types of display window units. The first is called the *closed* window design. In the closed window unit it is possible to separate completely the store's interior from the display window. This separation is made possible by a full background panel which encloses the entire back (and often the sides as well) of the window display unit. Major department stores often use this type of window. The advantage of the closed window is that the customer's full attention can be on the window. Also, the closed window can be located anywhere on the exterior of the store and would not need to be adjacent to a selling area.

A second type of unit is referred to as the *semiclosed* window. This unit has a half-panel background which allows customers to see over the displayed merchandise into the store. Drugstores, jewelry stores, and hardware stores are examples of retail operations that use semiclosed window units. The semiclosed unit allows some background for the window display but also allows customers to see into the store. Inside the store, space by the unit can be used for merchandise or display.

Illustration 19 The closed window unit is popular with department stores.

Illustration 20 The semiclosed window unit provides a partial background but also allows viewers to see into the store.

The third type of unit is the **open** window display. Since this type of window unit has no background panel, it is possible for the customer to look directly into the store. In effect, the whole store becomes part of the display window. Merchandise is shown being displayed on the counters and racks, in addition to any merchandise that may be shown in the window itself. This type of window display unit is popular in shopping malls and for large grocery stores.

Illustration 21 The open window unit allows the entire store to be on display.

USES OF WINDOW DISPLAYS

What are window displays used for? If you examine window presentations in a dozen different stores you might feel that you have seen a dozen different uses for window display. There is no question that windows are used in a variety of ways. Some of the more common or standard uses can be classified as described in the following material.

Related-Merchandise Displays

For all types of stores, one of the most popular uses for window display units is to present a collection of **related merchandise**. Properly arranged, this kind of visual presentation can be very effective. A typical related-merchandise window might contain a woman's dress, displayed on a mannequin, with related items such as purse, shoes, scarf, and jewelry correctly placed. A non-clothing related-merchandise window might include all of the items necessary to do a home painting job—paint, drop cloth, brushes, roller and roller pan, spackle, ladder, and even a cap.

Keep in mind that it is not necessary to display a central item in every related-merchandise presentation. Consider, for instance, a window containing winter-wear items. These could include slacks, sweaters, parkas, boots, and mittens. Although no one item may receive particular emphasis, this display would indeed be an example of a related-merchandise display.

Whether merchandise emphasis is used or not, the theme or purpose of the display should be very clear to the potential customer. Usually the relationship between related-merchandise items is clear. If not, a sign containing the theme should be made part of the window presentation. In the case of the winter wear mentioned earlier, a sign saying something like "Think Snow" might set forth an attention-getting theme, if one is needed.

Line-of-Goods Displays

Some retailers specialize in selling one kind of merchandise, such as shoes, bicycles, computers, or luggage. These retailers develop window presentations that can be described as containing a **line of goods**. For example, you probably have seen a window display containing a single brand of radios, television sets, and stereo equipment. More than likely, the manufacturer's name was displayed prominently, too. Even though different *kinds* of products were placed together, this display would be considered a line-of-goods window.

Line-of-goods displays are not limited to specialty stores. It is also possible for a large department store that carries the complete line of a nationally known manufacturer to use line-of-goods displays. Most often the line-of-goods display features one type of product but includes several brands and models of that item.

Mass Displays

In a **mass-display** window, merchandise fills the entire area. Often very little attention is given to the way in which various merchandise items are arranged, if indeed there is any basic arrangement

Illustration 22   A line-of-goods display can show several models of the same brand.

at all. The merchandise displayed may not even be related. In fact, a mass-display window often is the opposite of a well-designed display. In spite of this, there is a certain "magic" about mass-display windows. They communicate the impression of low prices and wide selection to the customer. Mass displays hold a particular appeal for the casual shopper who is looking for bargains. As a result, merchants who rely on price appeal to sell merchandise depend heavily on mass-display windows to bring customers into their stores. Variety stores, drugstores, discount stores, and food stores are among the main users of mass-display techniques.

Special-Event Displays

A **special-event** window, as the name indicates, is used to feature merchandise related to the event being celebrated. Examples of such events include store anniversaries, community recognition days, Easter, Christmas, Mother's Day, Father's Day, and special promotions such as "Back-to-School Days."

Sometimes the special-event window display carries a theme that is promoted throughout the entire store or shopping mall. Special-event windows always should be designed to bring customers into the store to buy as well as to call attention to a particular event. Thus, for an event such as Founder's Day, a window may feature a photo or news story from the founding date, but the window also would present merchandise items currently offered by the store.

Sale Displays

Window presentations of special-purchase, bargain, or clearance merchandise are called *sale displays*. Customers are attracted to this type of display because they are seeking bargains. They can be encouraged to come in to buy from stores that feature a good selection of merchandise at favorable prices. Sale displays are easy to notice because they often are trimmed with large and colorful banners and because special signs are used when a sale is taking place.

These five standard or common uses of display windows have unlimited variations depending upon the merchandise to be featured and the image desired by the store. In fact, the way in which windows may be used for the visual presentation of merchandise is limited only by the creativity and imagination of the display worker.

COMPONENTS OF A DISPLAY WINDOW

When display people refer to *components* they usually are referring to the various parts of the window unit and to the items used in the display. Windows used for visual presentations and the items used in the display have several components which can be identified in the following way:

1. Backgrounds
2. Floor coverings
3. Sides and ceilings
4. Merchandise
5. Lighting
6. Props
7. Signs.

Have you ever tried to put a picture puzzle together when a piece was missing? Window displays, like picture puzzles, are not complete if important pieces or components have been left out. Proper planning, along with some knowledge of how display planning components fit together, should prevent you from overlooking necessary components.

Backgrounds

A well-planned *background* is essential to a good window display. Contrasting backgrounds can emphasize merchandise lines, shapes, sizes, textures, weights, and colors. Usually, window display backgrounds are made of materials such as wallboard, various fabrics, corrugated board, wood panels, and fiberboard. Some of these backgrounds can be painted or covered with other materials as needed for each change of display.

Backgrounds can be the means of communicating display themes. A display of children's fall clothing placed in front of a school building scene is an example. When display windows are located side by side, different backgrounds can give each window its own identification, or theme. Extra care must be taken that such backgrounds do not draw attention away from the merchandise being displayed. Also, the effectiveness of backgrounds can be lost if they are not changed regularly.

Illustration 23   Through variations in the types of backgrounds used, windows can create a variety of visual impressions. Here several types of backgrounds are used in a single window.

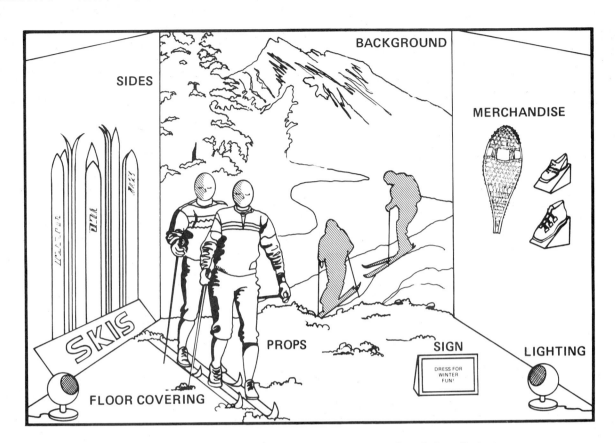

Figure 3-1 The preliminary sketch above includes all the components of a window display.

Floor Coverings

Although carpeting is the most popular covering for display unit floors, other **floor coverings** such as cork chips, sand, rocks, grass, or straw mats frequently are used to provide texture for a display design. Well-maintained hardwood flooring is often the base floor for many window units. Floor coverings should not in any way detract from the merchandise displayed. For that reason, neutral colors such as grays, blacks, or beiges often are used. Whatever the floor covering might be, it should be kept neat and clean.

Sides and Ceilings

When compared with other display components, **window unit sides and ceilings** may seem to be unimportant. Because these components typically are not in the customer's line of vision, they tend to be overlooked during the display planning stage. There are, however, two suggestions which should be kept in mind as you work with sides and ceilings. First, the ceiling and sides of a window unit should fit well with the background and the floor. Contrasts should not be permitted unless they serve a specific purpose, such as highlighting

certain items of merchandise. Second, display-unit ceilings and sides should be free of distracting objects such as loose wire, staples, hooks, tape, or even door handles. If a messy wall or ceiling is even slightly visible, it can spoil the overall effect of the visual presentation.

Merchandise

The most important component in any display is the **merchandise** — the goods offered for sale. No matter how much time is spent in preparing other window components, it will make little difference if the wrong merchandise is used. So it is essential that all merchandise intended for display in windows be chosen carefully. You can be fairly sure that merchandise choices will be correct if they have sales appeal, eye appeal, and time appeal. Because of the extreme importance of correct merchandise, specific techniques useful in selecting proper merchandise will be presented later in this section.

Lighting

Lighting effectiveness must be judged by its contribution to the merchandise presentation.

Proper lighting helps to enhance merchandise texture, color, and size. Variations in the brightness of the lights within the window unit make it possible to direct customer attention to specific items or features.

There are three basic lighting techniques which you can use to direct customer vision to the merchandise or to particular merchandise features. One technique is called *pinpointing*. A special lighting fixture with a very narrow beam is directed at the item to be featured. The narrow beam of light will emphasize that specific item. Jewelry, dishes, and silverware are examples of merchandise which can be displayed attractively in this manner.

Spotlighting is another useful lighting technique. As the name implies, spotlights are used to focus customer attention on spots, either merchandise or areas, within the window. Spotlights are effective with large merchandise items such as appliances, sporting goods, and furniture.

A third technique, *floodlighting*, is very useful when an entire window display, rather than individual items, is used to attract shoppers. Floodlights usually are recessed in the ceiling of the display unit and are directed over the entire presentation area. Floodlights can work well with many types of merchandise and in combination with pinpoints and spots.

As you gain experience in display design and construction, you will realize that most window units are underlighted. It is true, however, that too much light can "wash out" the merchandise. The amount of light needed will be determined by the colors of the window background and the merchandise. Light colors reflect light, so less lighting is needed when the unit is trimmed in light colors. Dark colors absorb light, so more lighting will be needed when background and merchandise are in the darker colors. Colored lights also can be used to create interesting contrasts between the merchandise and the window unit itself.

Whatever type of lighting is used, light fixtures should be out of the customer's direct line of vision as much as possible. Light fixtures may be placed behind props or merchandise or may be attached to the ceiling of the unit. Extreme care should be taken to make sure that flammable items are not placed against light fixtures. Also, heat generated by the lights, and sometimes added to by direct sunlight, can raise the temperature inside the window very rapidly. Therefore, proper ventilation of the window unit is an important consideration when lighting is being planned. Because display and store lighting is an area requiring special skills, persons interested in knowing more should refer to the additional resources on lighting listed in the Selected References section of this book.

Props

Fixtures used in displays to physically support or hold merchandise are called *functional props*. Functional props include items such as panels, screens, pedestals, tables, stands, mannequins, shirt and blouse forms, and T bars. All of these items are referred to as *standard props*. They are so named because each is commonly used and can be purchased from any number of display-fixture manufacturers. In smaller stores where money for prop purchases is limited, it may be necessary to build the props that are needed.

In addition to the functional props, other items are used in display to add color, texture, or theme. These props are called *decorative props* and include items such as sea shells, watering cans, art objects, antique chairs, plants, and pottery. Decorative props are used to carry out the theme or develop the setting of the display.

As you gain display design experience, you will discover that finding good props is not difficult if you know where to hunt for them. Garage sales, attics, basements, and flea markets are a few of the possible sources. You might even swap props with other businesses. Through the use of imagination you can come up with all kinds of ideas that will not cost much and may add considerably to the effectiveness of a visual presentation.

Whether props are bought or made, they must be adequate to the job. Since many props are not completely covered by the merchandise being displayed, it is important that their condition and finish be appropriate to the display design. Props that are chipped, scratched, or broken will detract from the display's visual impression. Careful storage of props between uses is necessary to protect them from damage and dust.

Signs

Window *signs* provide information that otherwise might not be communicated to the customer. Display themes, prices, sizes, product features, and location of the merchandise in the store are examples of information that can be provided by window signs. Signs need to be used carefully and in a manner that will not detract from the display. Signs that are poorly designed or badly placed can ruin your best display efforts. Suggestions

Illustration 24 Careful choice of props can help a display person show merchandise in an effective manner. Can you identify the standard props used here? Which of these props would be considered decorative?

for proper sign layout and use are presented in Section 4.

SELECTING MERCHANDISE FOR DISPLAY

Choosing the correct merchandise for presentation is one of the most important decisions you will make in designing and constructing a window display. No matter how attractive your displays are, they will not produce sales if poorly selected merchandise is featured. Many factors affect the choice of merchandise for window presentations but three features tend to be present in most

successful choices. Appropriate merchandise has (1) sales appeal, (2) time appeal, and (3) eye appeal.

Merchandise with Sales Appeal

You probably know of some retailers who have made the mistake of using their window units to promote leftover merchandise, buyers' mistakes, or other items the retailer desperately wanted to get rid of. Experience over time has shown that no amount of advertising, display, or other promotion will get customers to buy goods they do not want. Displaying items that have little customer interest is a sure way to cause people to lose interest in a store. Windows should be used only for merchandise that has proven sales appeal—items that are in a category of "best sellers." When considering merchandise for window display ask yourself, Is this item going to have a strong sales appeal for most of the potential customers who pass by?

Merchandise with Time Appeal

Customers who always are interested in new items, the latest fashions, and improved products are said to be interested in the timeliness of the product. Other customers tend to be interested in goods only when those goods are seasonal. For example, most customers buy holiday cards in the weeks just ahead of the holiday. Offering such cards at other times of the year probably would result in few sales. Both of these cases involve time appeal— new, up-to-date, improved, and seasonal items. Timely merchandise often is tied in with important national or local events, moods about the weather, changing seasons, or current fashions.

To make your displays timely, you must give attention to merchandise that is making news. Most importantly, you must be willing to change window presentations quickly in order to take advantage of current customer interests. If you are alert to changing customer interests you will have a better chance of producing displays that sell more merchandise. Few features of a window presentation are more important than the timeliness of the merchandise.

Merchandise with Eye Appeal

The most useful items are not always the most attractive. For instance, nothing is more useful, on certain occasions, than a mop. But a window full of mops is not likely to have strong visual appeal for most customers.

Items should be placed in a window because of their attractive appearance, timeliness, or special customer interest. Merchandise on hand or soon to be received always should be reviewed for these characteristics. Of the potential best sellers that are timely, some are bound to have more eye appeal than others. Those are the items that should be selected for presentation in a window unit.

BUILDING EFFECTIVE WINDOW DISPLAYS

The actual steps followed in planning and constructing window displays vary from store to store.

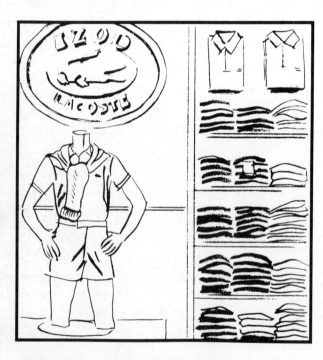

Figure 3-2 A well-designed window starts with a sketch showing the theme and indicating how the various window components will be used in the visual presentation. Identify the components shown here.

Illustration 25 The effective window presentation will have sales appeal, time appeal, and eye appeal. Note the simple and dramatic use of the sign in this semiclosed window.

Such things as store size, types of merchandise sold, and display policies are important factors in deciding the exact display-planning and display-building techniques to use. But regardless of these variations, certain steps are fundamental to both the planning and the installation of window displays.

Planning the Window Presentation

Promotional themes often are established well in advance of the time when work actually begins on displays. Each display plan should include the promotional theme and some ideas on how merchandise, props, lighting, and signs can be combined to carry out that theme. The display begins to take form with the sketch of the proposed merchandise arrangement. Questions such as the following need to be answered as the planning proceeds:

1. How can this be done not only to feature the merchandise but also to express the character of the store?
2. How can human interest be worked into this display? Can the articles be displayed so that they suggest use by the customer?
3. Can this display be tied in with local or regional events or seasonal needs?
4. Can this display be tied in with the store's local or national advertising?
5. What colors and lighting would be most appropriate to the theme and the goods featured?

Without consideration of questions such as these, many opportunities for effective display may be overlooked. After the sketch is roughed out, a list of merchandise items, props, signs, lighting, and other materials should be prepared. From these lists work may begin or orders may be placed so that necessary items will be ready by the installation date. This planning process needs to be done for each and every window display to be installed.

Installing the Window Presentation

The installation of a window display should be done as quickly as possible. Valuable promotional time is lost during every minute that a window stands empty. The following installation routine can reduce the time needed to build a display by eliminating unnecessary motion and effort.

1. Place a screen or draw a curtain to close off the window. Then the installation will not detract from other displays. Also, if you close off the unit, you will have a better chance of completing the display without interruption.
2. Remove all merchandise from the props and

fixtures. In some cases store policy will require that mannequins be taken to a display work area before merchandise is removed. Fold any clothing items or place them on hangers. Merchandise should be prepared for return to the various departments or buyers' offices, where it will be returned to stock.
3. Remove all props and fixtures from the window and load them onto stock trucks for return to the display department. If certain props or fixtures are needed for the new display, set them aside for return to the window.
4. Wash window glass; sweep and/or vacuum the floor; clean the background, sides, and ceiling of the unit; and remove nails, staples, and other evidence of the previous display.
5. Replace light bulbs or tubes as necessary. Move lighting fixtures if a new location is required in the upcoming display.
6. Place props for the new display in the window area according to the display sketch. Usually it is best to start with the larger props and then arrange the smaller ones. If the window unit is deep or long, the order in which items are moved in is important for a quick installation.
7. Bring the merchandise into the window area and place it on appropriate props according to the display plan. When convenient, arrange merchandise on display forms in the display department work area before bringing them to the display unit.
8. Bring in accessory merchandise and decorative props to give the window the finishing touch.
9. Place window signs and individual merchandise tickets in the appropriate spots. Set the lighting according to the display plan and check to make sure that it works.
10. Check the window to see that your plan is complete. Remove all unnecessary items and tools. Remove the curtain or screen. View the window from the outside to make sure all details are correct.

Without careful attention to these steps, the display will take extra time to install. In addition, the quality of the display may be lower than you would like it to be.

Safety Considerations

Reasonable care and good judgement can prevent personal accidents and damage to the merchandise and the window unit. There are certain things in particular you should guard against.

Fire is the greatest hazard in display building.

Frayed wiring, overloaded electric circuits or motors, and materials (even though treated) all can be flammable, so all problems should be eliminated before damage occurs. Care also should be taken not to place merchandise near spotlights or heat-generating fixtures.

Remember that one side of the window display is made of glass. A careless sharp bump or the impact of merchandise falling against the glass could be disastrous. Window glass always should be treated with caution.

Staples and nails often are used in display work. Sometimes all of them are not removed when a display is being changed. Remember that sharp points and nail heads could cause serious cuts and scratches. It is simply good practice to be extra careful when removing these hazards while cleaning the window area in preparation for a new display.

Accidents also occur as a result of mishandling props, merchandise, and work equipment. All of these accidents can be avoided if reasonable care is taken and if regular attention is given to proper procedures during the preparation and installation of the display.

SUMMARY

The purpose of good window displays is to sell merchandise. The retailer who uses window presentations of merchandise expects passersby to notice what is featured and then come into the store to examine the goods and, hopefully, to buy. Window units can be fully closed, semiclosed, or open. They may be used for showing related goods, a line of goods, mass displays, goods tied to special events, or sale goods.

The components of a window unit and the items shown combine to make a visual presentation that will enhance the merchandise and provide a desired impression of the store. The selection of the correct merchandise for a window presentation is an important decision in the planning of a display window. Merchandise for display can be judged by its sales appeal, time appeal, and eye appeal. Good window planning is necessary to achieve the desired results, and a standard procedure for installation is important if displays are to be set up promptly. Safety is always an important consideration in any display installation.

4. INTERIOR DISPLAY PRESENTATIONS

The purpose of this section and related projects is to help students:

- Understand the importance of interior displays in modern merchandising.
- Identify the difference between open and closed interior displays.
- Describe specific kinds of interior displays and their various uses.
- Select interior display merchandise and appropriate display units.
- Identify "best locations" for the various kinds of interior displays.
- Make use of the various display elements and principles in designing interior display arrangements.
- Understand, design, and make effective interior display signs.

Retailing changes rapidly! Like many other aspects of American business, today's retail merchandising practices have changed greatly in recent years. For instance, there was a time when customers could not select purchases without the help of a salesperson. This help was called *wait-on service*. Because most merchandise was not packaged for immediate sale, it had to be kept in closed display cases in the store. The retailer had no choice but to use wait-on service to take care of customer needs. Now, the use of interior displays for direct selling has changed all that.

INTERIOR DISPLAYS AND MODERN MERCHANDISING

Modern merchandising techniques make wait-on service almost unnecessary today. Through the use of effective advertising, modern packaging, and self-selection, store interior displays have become a major means of making merchandise more accessible to customers.

Retailers know that customers often are well informed about many products before entering a store to shop. Advertising promotions through newspapers, television, radio, and direct mail have had a great deal to do with increased product knowledge on the part of customers. Good exterior window displays and certain kinds of point-of-purchase displays also have become an effective way to presell specific merchandise. As a result, interior displays have become an important part of retail merchandising plans.

Advertising and window displays have not been the only factors contributing to an increase in the use of interior store displays. New and attractive product-packaging techniques also have made it possible to use more interior display units. Display personnel now are able to exhibit merchandise openly in a variety of interior display arrangements not possible before. Food, clothing, and hardware are just a few examples of products that formerly required a salesperson's assistance to be sold. Presenting prepackaged merchandise on interior displays allows customers to have direct access to a wide selection of goods. This kind of merchandising is called *self-service retailing*.

Interior display units also have proved to be an effective means of selling goods that are not prepackaged. Interior units allow the customer to inspect merchandise firsthand. This experience often results in a sale. Market studies dealing with buying habits show that customers purchase many items on impulse, that is, they buy without planning to do so in advance. To encourage impulse buying, the merchant must (1) make merchandise visible, (2) make it attractive, (3) show it in use, and (4) make it accessible. Interior display is, without a doubt, one of the most effective ways of motivating the customer to make a purchase.

KINDS OF INTERIOR DISPLAYS

You probably have noticed the wide variety of interior displays that are used to sell merchandise. For the most part, units of this kind can be

Illustration 26   The decision by the merchant to emphasize personal (wait-on) selling or to depend on various kinds of interior displays to promote sales is influenced by the products being sold and the desired store image.

described as being either open or closed displays.

Merchandise in an **open** display is placed on tables, counter tops, or racks, or in bins. This makes it possible for the customer to inspect and handle the merchandise without a salesperson's assistance.

Some merchandise needs to be protected in **closed case** displays where customers can see but not handle it. Jewelry, fine silver, and certain unpackaged food items are examples of goods that must be covered for protection against damage, theft, or contamination. Obviously the use of closed cases is more expensive than the use of open displays. However, closed display can add prestige to the displayed items if the display case and lighting are designed to increase merchandise appeal.

There are several specific types of open and closed display units. Among the types most commonly used are island, end, platform, shadow box, background, and point-of-purchase interior displays.

Island

Island displays, sometimes referred to as **gondolas**, often are designed through the use of large, open display tables stacked high with sale or featured merchandise. This kind of display may be approached from all sides. It is most effective when located in heavy customer-traffic areas. Department, food, and specialty stores rely heavily on island displays in their sales promotions.

End

An **end** display is usually an open display of merchandise on a rack or table or in a bin, located at the end of a merchandise aisle. Supermarkets and discount retailers make extensive use of end displays to promote the sale of specially priced, new, or seasonal merchandise. Often, end-display merchandise also can be found in its regular stock location. Customers who fail to see it there, however, will seldom miss seeing that same merchandise if it is located on an end display.

Platform

Some open displays make use of raised **platforms** placed on the floor of the store. Furniture, appliances, and similar items can be presented very effectively through platform display. Featured clothing, shown on full-size mannequins, typically is displayed in this manner. A major feature of this type of display is the elevation of displayed items above surrounding merchandise. Platform displays are excellent attention-getters. For this reason they often are located near a store's main entrance or in view of heavy traffic areas leading to key departments.

Shadow Box

A **shadow box** is an enclosed display box built into a wall or placed on a counter or ledge. Customers usually are not able to handle merchandise

Illustration 27   Open interior displays make it possible for customers to inspect at firsthand the merchandise that is on display. Closed interior displays are designed to present merchandise in an attractive fashion without permitting product access by customers.

displayed in this way. Shadow boxes are most effective when used to highlight special merchandise. Gloves, purses, jewelry, shirts, ties, shoes, and other small items are good choices for this kind of display unit. To add to the effect, indirect lighting may be used inside the shadow box itself. This lighting should be brighter than surrounding light so that the display will attract customer attention.

Background

Background interior displays make use of store walls, ledges, wall shelves, and partitions. This type of display can be either open or closed. Background displays make it possible for the display builder to use interior space that otherwise might not be noticed. Because background displays usually are placed above eye level, motion, color, and lighting are important factors in drawing customer attention. Quite often, such displays present merchandise and decorations related to a store-wide theme.

Point-of-Purchase

Point-of-purchase displays often are provided by manufacturers to promote their products. Depending on the type of product to be displayed, such displays can be designed for open or closed use.

Because these displays are convenient to set up, their use is increasing rapidly in department stores, discount stores, and supermarkets. In most cases, all a display person needs to do is decide where the point-of-purchase display should be located. The unit usually is designed, delivered, and sometimes set up by the representative of the manufacturer whose products are being displayed. The display often comes with specific product advertising printed directly on the unit, thus eliminating the need to make display signs.

Point-of-purchase displays are attractive and easy to care for and are designed to promote self-service. The only disadvantage of point-of-purchase units is that they are constructed to sell only one line of merchandise. But they do sell merchandise well, and that is the real test of a good interior display. Because point-of-purchase displays have become one of the most popular and effective means of selling large-volume, fast-moving merchandise, they will be discussed in greater detail in Section 5.

INTERIOR DISPLAY FUNDAMENTALS

Ask retailers which displays sell the most merchandise. Chances are they will tell you that interior displays do the best job. They also may say that interior displays create traffic, give the customer

Illustration 28 Above are examples of island, end, and platform displays. You should be able to identify each of these easily.

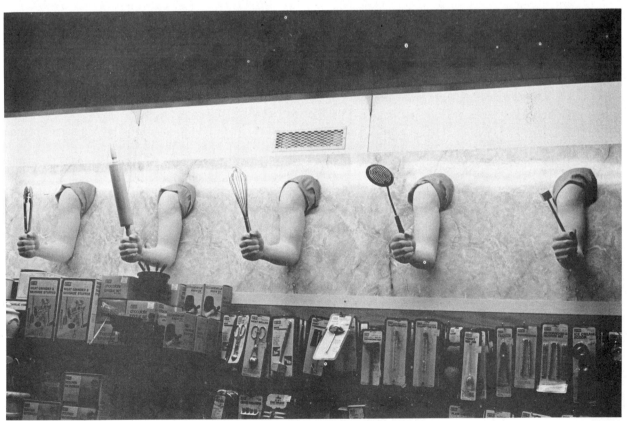

Illustration 29 Above are examples of shadow box, point-of-purchase, and background displays. Note how each type utilizes a different sort of space to carry its sales message.

direct contact with the merchandise, and cut selling costs. No wonder interior displays are popular with merchants and customers!

Do not assume that all interior displays work perfectly, however. Some do a poor job of selling merchandise. Usually this is because one or more of the important interior display fundamentals have been overlooked. Remember, planning prevents failure. It is necessary to select appropriate merchandise, to use the right type of display unit, to locate the display in a suitable place, to arrange the display effectively, and to use signs properly. Consider the following suggestions as you plan and construct your own interior displays.

Selecting Interior Display Merchandise

Merchandise is the key! Remember, the merchandise must have sales, eye, and time appeal. And it must fit, both in size and shape, the display unit in which it is being placed. Proper merchandise selection is fundamental to the success of any interior display.

Effective merchandise displays can build customer traffic. In fact, they may be used to attract customers to areas of the store where slower selling merchandise is located. For displays to do this, however, they must feature merchandise that has strong customer appeal. Sometimes interior displays containing less-well-known merchandise will succeed in increasing sales of that merchandise. In most cases, however, "best seller" products should be used when the purpose of the interior display is to create customer traffic. Asking the advice of departmental sales staff, and possibly checking accounting records, can help you choose "best seller" merchandise.

The sales appeal of certain items or lines of merchandise often is created by national, regional, and local advertising programs. It takes the local store display person, however, to finish the sales-promotion job. Top-notch window and interior displays must be designed to feature the merchandise that is being advertised. Customers expect these display services, and they look for them.

Advertising brings customers to the store. Window displays provide the first real look at advertised merchandise. But it takes a good interior display to close the sale. For a sale to happen, merchandise must be available to the customer for inspection. Interior displays are designed to allow and encourage such inspection.

Choosing Interior Display Units

Interior display units are designed to attract customers and to sell merchandise. These units work best when they (1) present high-demand, attractively priced merchandise, (2) are placed in appropriate store locations, and (3) are changed regularly in order to draw the attention of both regular and new customers.

Remember that the merchandise is most important to the success of a display. But choosing the display unit carelessly can reduce the sales appeal of almost any merchandise display. Keep in mind the following guidelines when making interior display unit choices:

1. Select only those display units that can present the major features of the merchandise effectively.
2. Where practical, choose interior display units that allow customers to inspect merchandise closely and select the items they want.
3. Avoid using display units so brightly colored that they take attention away from the merchandise on display.
4. Make sure that each display unit is properly lighted. Where regular store lighting is not bright enough, use units that have self-contained lighting.
5. Use caution in placing display units in areas where they may disrupt or block traffic. Interior displays should encourage, not discourage, customer traffic.
6. Dividers, shelves, or partitions should be used when more than one kind of merchandise is placed on a single display unit.
7. To prevent accidents or damage, check the construction of each interior display fixture to make sure it will accommodate the size, shape, and weight of the merchandise to be placed on it.

Locating Interior Displays

Some retailers make the mistake of putting their best-sellers in the best location—near the front of the store. When best-selling merchandise is displayed in the best location, traffic flow in the store is often bunched up in a small area. The result is that less popular merchandise may sell more slowly because customers do not have to go by it. The goal of every display person should be to place interior displays in such a way that traffic flows evenly throughout the store.

Properly located, interior displays can sell both fast- and slow-moving merchandise. For example,

Illustration 30   Interior displays are most effective when they are coordinated with the merchant's advertising efforts and window displays.

imagine that you place an interior display containing fast-selling picnic supplies near a display of slow-moving garden hoses. Chances are that the increased traffic created by the picnic supply display will cause more customers to stop and look at the garden hose display. Not only is it located nearby, but it is seasonally related to backyard picnics. This increased exposure could mean increased sales of garden hose.

Display space is valuable and often limited. Therefore, it should be used to best advantage. There are a number of "best spot" locations for interior displays in a retail store. These locations vary, depending on the type and size of the store being

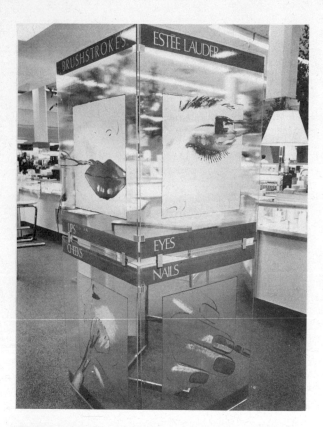

Illustration 31 The proper placement of interior displays is a key factor in drawing customer traffic through the store.

considered. Here are some standard interior display locations that work for most retailers:

1. Just inside the front doors
2. At the ends of aisles
3. Opposite service counters
4. Near checkout counters
5. Across from elevators and escalators
6. Next to related items
7. In front of open window displays
8. In front of entrances to departments.

Designing Interior Display Arrangements

There may be a certain amount of luck involved in creating display arrangements that sell merchandise. Most display designers, however, depend on their knowledge of display elements and principles in order to do the job correctly. You will recall that design elements and principles were discussed earlier, in Section 2. Display design elements include (1) line, (2) shape, (3) size, (4) weight, (5) texture, and (6) color. These elements are used to describe the optical effect of both merchandise and display

units. Principles of display design, which deal with the placement of merchandise in a display unit, include (1) harmony, (2) contrast, (3) emphasis, (4) proportion, and (5) balance (formal and informal).

If you were to compare various kinds of interior display units from store to store, probably you would find very few differences in fixture designs. Islands, platforms, and end units, for example, would be nearly alike. This does not mean, though, that the merchandising arrangements in those units would also be similar. Section 2 also explained a variety of ways in which display merchandise might be arranged. A review of those basic arrangements may help you come up with an idea based on repetition, step or zigzag formation, pyramidal shape, or radiating (wheel) design. The type of merchandise to be displayed, along with the number and kinds of interior display props available, also will influence your arrangement choices.

Signs in Interior Displays

Signs, or *show cards*, act as silent salespeople for interior merchandise displays. That is, signs provide the kinds of information customers need in order to make their buying decisions. Details such as sizes, styles, colors, prices, and major product features often are included in sign copy. The success of self-service retailing depends in part on this kind of information being readily available to customers. Without it, neither interior displays nor self-service merchandising will achieve maximum results.

Illustration 32 The appearance and copy content of a sign may encourage customers to examine merchandise more carefully and perhaps to make a purchase.

Because interior display signs are limited in size, the information they contain must be brief and to the point. A typical layout for a display sign would include (1) a headline identifying the product, (2) brief copy listing major product features, and (3) the price of the merchandise. Signs should contain information that anticipates and answers customer questions about the merchandise. For instance, consider a display of sport shirts and matching slacks. Experience tells us that our customers will want to know if this merchandise can be washed or must be dry cleaned. This is the kind of information that should be included on the sign. Anticipating customers' questions saves time and helps make self-service merchandising work.

Customers seldom give more than a passing glance to small interior display show cards. For this reason, the lettering on the sign should stand out. It should, in fact, appear to jump right off the signboard. For example, black or red letters on a white signboard will gain attention through contrast. Lettering should be large enough to be read by customers who pass by the display at a distance. Easily read, high-contrast signs can attract customers who otherwise might ignore the display.

Finally, all store signs must be kept in good condition. Signs that are soiled or torn are worse than no signs at all. Changing signs frequently can help to keep needed display information fresh and attractive.

EFFECTIVE INTERIOR DISPLAYS IN REVIEW

Interior display space is costly. It has been estimated that interior display space in department stores costs a minimum of $4,000 annually per six-foot display unit. To get that money back in increased sales requires effective interior displays. Both in large and in small stores, care must be taken to see that space occupied by interior displays is well used.

It takes time and experience to learn all the "tricks of the trade" for designing interior displays that increase sales. There are, however, basic rules that can help you avoid making serious interior display errors. Some of these rules are as follows:

- Use only merchandise that is fresh and in good condition.
- Choose interior display units that fit the product and that will serve as handy dispensers of merchandise.

- Put emphasis on the merchandise by means of high-intensity lighting, or through strong contrasts in display elements such as color, shape, or size.
- Place interior displays so that customer traffic will be drawn through the store in a systematic way.
- When possible, place major display items at eye level so that customers will see them easily.
- Use signs suggesting reasons why the customer should buy displayed items.
- When price is important, use large, bold figures on display signs.
- When manufacturers' point-of-purchase materials are available, use them to create variety in your displays.
- Change displays frequently so that customers always will find new and interesting merchandise to look at — and buy.
- Select interior display fixtures and props that are flexible and easily stored. Keep them in good condition.

Interior displays, like window displays, require planning and organization in advance of their installation. Taking this into consideration as you design and build interior displays can pay off in increased sales for your store.

SUMMARY

Interior displays often are a reflection of a store's method of doing business. Because great emphasis now is being placed on self-service retailing, interior displays play a major role in attracting and directing customer attention. Most importantly, interior display presentations are a major means of selling merchandise.

Commonly used interior display units include the island, end, platform, shadow box, background, and point-of-purchase units. Depending on the type of merchandise being presented, these displays can be designed as closed cases or to provide access for customers. Skilled display designers know that proper merchandise selection, care in choosing display locations, and continuous unit maintenance (including merchandise replacement) also will increase the effectiveness of any interior display. Application of the display elements and principles reviewed in Section 2 and careful use of signs or show cards in interior display units will make such units an effective means of increasing sales.

5. POINT-OF-PURCHASE PRESENTATIONS

The purpose of this section and related projects is to help students:

- Define point-of-purchase displays.
- Explain how point-of-purchase presentations are used.
- Describe the various types of point-of-purchase presentation units.
- Select the appropriate type of point-of-purchase unit to meet a specific merchandising need.
- Explain how point-of-purchase presentations can be used effectively to sell merchandise.
- Explain the benefits to retailers of a shelf management system.
- Identify sources of point-of-purchase presentation materials.

Even a well-planned promotional campaign with good window and interior displays may not be enough to help assure successful sales! In fact, recent marketing studies show that as many as 80 percent of consumers buy on impulse. That is, they purchase products they had not planned to buy before entering the store. In order to attract these customers, most retailers make use of point-of-purchase displays.

Point-of-purchase displays are a specialized form of visual merchandising planned to reach customers who make rapid buying decisions. Displays of this type are designed to be attention getting so they will spark impulse sales. To create exciting displays, designers utilize lighting, sound, animation, color, and unique construction materials. Some point-of-purchase display units, such as motorized and lighted counter cases for watches, are created for years of use. Others— such as brightly colored cardboard units containing seasonal merchandise —are intended only for temporary use. Without point-of-purchase displays, retailers would lose one of their strongest selling tools—the opportunity to grab customers' attention while they are in the store.

POINT-OF-PURCHASE USES

The Point of Purchase Advertising Institute (POPAI) has found that, in general, retailers want point-of-purchase displays (POP's) that will (1) gain customer attention, (2) clearly identify the product, (3) provide product information, and (4) motivate the customer to buy. Retailers also prefer display units that can be used for a particular merchandising function. Brief descriptions of some possible uses for POP's are given in the following paragraphs.

Advertising Function

Displays designed to carry out an *advertising function* do not contain the product being promoted. Instead, they are supposed to inform and remind. They accomplish this through the use of illustrations which will enhance the merchandise's image. Examples of POP's with an advertising function include signs indicating that certain credit cards will be accepted; lighted units identifying in-store specials; and signs picturing particular products and describing their features and serviceability.

Selling Function

Point-of-purchase displays designed to carry out a *selling function* do contain the product being promoted. Customers cannot take products from this unit, but they are able to see the actual merchandise and to obtain key information. Some examples of POP's with a selling function are a display for power saws which presents information on how the saw operates and on safety and mechanical features; a shampoo display which gives details on a new PH factor or anti-dandruff ingredient; and a tester for cologne which allows the customer to sample the product.

Merchandising Function

A point-of-purchase display with a **merchandising function** is one from which shoppers can actually purchase the product. Toothpaste displays, candy displays, pen and pencil displays, and film displays provide familiar examples of this type of display.

Incentive Program and Promotion Function

Displays that contain premium offers, dealer incentives, sweepstakes entry forms, recipe offers, or coupons are displays which carry out an **incentive program and promotion function**. They are designed to promote certain products. Examples of point-of-purchase displays used for this function include racks containing samples of food spices and recipes for their use, audio-visual presentations of products, and displays containing product pictures and registration forms for customer sweepstakes entries.

Regardless of their intended use, point-of-purchase displays ultimately must be judged on how well they sell products, services, and ideas. Successful results are attained when appropriate display elements and principles are applied in the display unit's design.

POINT-OF-PURCHASE DISPLAY UNITS

Point-of-purchase displays vary widely in design and construction. In some cases, features of several types of units may be combined to create a new and different display. However, there are several basic and easy-to-recognize types of point-of-purchase display units which can be found in most retail stores. Among these are (1) counter units, (2) sales register units, (3) floorstand units, (4) freestanding pole units, (5) shelf units, (6) tester units, (7) wall units, (8) full-line merchandiser units, (9) incentive and premium units, and (10) sign units. Remember that a particular *unit* may be used for different *functions* at various times and in various stores.

Counter Units

Counter units are most effective when used to display fast-moving convenience goods such as candy, tobacco, and health and beauty aids. The best locations for such displays are in heavy traffic areas where highly visible counter space is available. Often a counter unit will come to the retailer in prepackaged form. That is, the merchandise already has been placed in or attached to the display unit by the manufacturer.

Sales Register Units

As their name implies, **sales register units** are designed to be attached to or placed near sales registers. Racks or small shelf displays commonly are used for this purpose. Checkout lanes are excellent display locations because of the high level of impulse buying that occurs while customers are waiting for service. In grocery stores, items such as gum and magazines frequently are located in sales register units.

Floorstand Units

Floorstand units are intended to separate certain items from other merchandise. They often are multi-sided for convenient customer access and they are large enough to be seen easily. Although floorstand units can be located anywhere in a retail store, they are most likely to be found at the ends of shopping aisles or near the entrances to various departments. They frequently contain featured or highly advertised merchandise such as light bulbs, hosiery, or greeting cards.

Freestanding Pole Units

Like floorstand units, **freestanding pole units** can be located anywhere on the selling floor. As their name implies, they are pole shaped, and they have hooks or racks upon which merchandise can be placed. Typically this kind of point-of-purchase display is used to present a single product, such as film or batteries.

Shelf Units

Ease of installation, low cost, and simple maintenance make point-of-purchase **shelf units** very popular among retailers. Shelf units are attached directly to existing store shelving and can be placed

Advertising Function

Merchandising Function

Selling Function

Incentive Program and Promotion Function

Illustration 33 Point-of-purchase displays can be used to advertise, to sell, or to merchandise a product, or to make special promotional offers.

wherever space is available. The flexibility of this display unit style with regard to location and size makes it possible to use shelf units to present a single product or a complete line of merchandise. In grocery stores, items such as spices, tea, or drink mixes can be featured through the use of shelf units.

Tester Units

Point-of-purchase **tester units** provide customers with an opportunity to try a product in the store before buying it. Food, mechanical or electronic toys, and toiletries often are promoted in this fashion. Some tester units hold both the samples and merchandise that can be purchased. Other tester units simply display samples of the product and are located near the regular display of the product. In either case, point-of-purchase tester units must be eye catching and must provide for easy customer access to the sample merchandise.

Wall Units

Wall units make it possible for retailers to utilize unused wall space for display purposes. Most wall units are designed to be attached directly to walls. Because of their size, however, some units are placed on the floor against an open wall area. All types of products can be promoted in this fashion, and it is to the retailer's advantage to use these units to gain additional display space in the store. In variety stores, items such as picture frames, mirrors, curtain rods, and drapery hardware often are displayed in wall units.

Full-Line Merchandiser Units

Full-line merchandiser units are intended to provide a single selling area for one manufacturer's products. Whether freestanding or attached to store fixtures, such units are recognized easily by customers because of their distinctive colors, merchandise arrangements, size, and identifying signs. Several varieties or styles of a single brand of gloves, knitwear, or cosmetics may be displayed in a full-line merchandiser unit.

Incentive and Premium Units

Among the most common and inexpensive types of point-of-purchase displays are the **incentive and premium units**. Used to promote all types of merchandise, these displays usually consist of cardboard signs or holders with tear-off coupons or

premium slips. These units may be attached to other types of point-of-purchase units or may be placed wherever available space exists.

Sign Units

Point-of-purchase **sign units** are used primarily to attract customers' attention and to direct them to product locations. Point-of-purchase signs are constructed of cardboard, metal, wood, or plastic. Some are lighted, while others may have moveable parts. They may direct customers to paint departments, shoe departments, or the locations of other well-known brand name merchandise. Most are brilliantly colored, contain only a small amount of copy, and emphasize the product's name. Depending on their design, point-of-purchase signs can be placed inside or outside the store. Some possible locations include other display units, walls, windows, parking lots, exterior walls, and store marquees.

POINT-OF-PURCHASE DESIGN SYSTEMS

Point-of-purchase display designers generally agree that there is an increasing need to provide display materials that will help the retailer better organize the rapidly growing number of products offered for sale. To accomplish this task, more and more point-of-purchase displays are being designed to departmentalize and compartmentalize merchandise. The Point of Purchase Advertising Institute has identified four point-of-purchase design systems currently being used to help merchants organize and present their merchandise effectively. These four are the shelf management, frame-out, air space, and boutique display systems. Each system may utilize one or more of the point-of-purchase *units* previously discussed. The following paragraphs briefly outline the main features of each system.

Shelf Management System

The **shelf management system** is used where certain products on a shelf may look confusing to the customer, as when there are a number of sizes, styles, or uses for the same line of products. First-aid products, for instance, tend to sell much better when a shelf management system is used. Such a system consists of plastic or wooden shelf extenders and dividers and of signs identifying individual

Illustration 34   Shown here are five types of point-of-purchase display units: counter, sales register, floorstand, freestanding pole, and shelf. Examine the photos above to identify each type.

Illustration 35 These photographs show examples of a full-line merchandiser unit, an incentive and premium unit, a tester unit, a wall unit, and a sign unit.

assortments of the products. Shelf management display systems also prove effective when used with beverages, household items, hardware, batteries, and similar items. The shelf management point-of-purchase system is popular with retailers because it provides several important benefits: (1) visual attractiveness, (2) easier stocking and inventory, and (3) increased customer awareness (impulse buying).

Frame-out System

The *frame-out system* is designed to outline a section of shelving which contains an entire product category. It creates a mini-department within a specific area where the product is normally stocked. To accomplish this effect, metal or plastic frames are attached directly to existing shelving around the merchandise being promoted. Wooden, metal, or plastic signs identifying the merchandise often are attached to the framing in order to draw attention to the display. A merchant may use this type of system to identify a specific line of merchandise, such as hosiery, or to draw attention to various brands of coffee placed together in a single location. In most instances, frame-outs are located within the store's shopping aisles rather than on the ends of rows or on freestanding display fixtures.

Air Space System

Display space on the sales floor in most retail stores has become crowded. To help solve this problem, point-of-purchase display designers have "taken to the air." That is, they are looking for ways to utilize unused and potentially valuable display space. The *air space system* makes use of overhead or above-counter space. Air space systems installed at or near checkout counters have proven most successful. Point-of-purchase displays of this kind usually involve building up from a counter top or building down from the ceiling. Plastic counter racks or ceiling poles with hooks or platforms are typical air space display components. Air space systems are most effective in presenting impulse-buying merchandise such as candy, potato chips, sun glasses, and other low-priced seasonal items.

Boutique System

The *boutique system* allows products to be departmentalized and displayed effectively through the use of many point-of-purchase display units. Freestanding displays and displays placed at the ends of shopping aisles often are used in the boutique system. A single unit may function as a vacationwear display and contain sunglasses, swimsuits, beach towels, and tote bags. The intent is to provide the feeling associated with a small specialty store. Several styles or brands of one product or an entire line of related products will be displayed in each one of the units. The customer can recognize, compare, and select products easily. The retailer benefits because boutique displays provide for greater inventory control, product emphasis, improved store appearance, and increased sales and profits.

OBTAINING POINT-OF-PURCHASE DISPLAY MATERIALS

Most point-of-purchase display materials found in retail stores are designed and constructed by professional display manufacturers. In a very few instances displays of this type are retailer-created. In most cases the merchant's best source of point-of-purchase display materials will be those firms that provide the merchandise the retailer sells. In fact, it is not unusual for product manufacturers to deliver and even set up point-of-purchase units that promote their products.

Depending on cost, some point-of-purchase displays simply are given to the retailer. This is usually the case with displays constructed of corrugated cardboard or similar inexpensive material. Some displays, however, must be purchased by the retailer, especially those that are intended for permanent use and are costly to design and construct. Normally, point-of-purchase displays of this kind are made of plastic, wire, wood, or metal. In addition, they frequently are lighted and may have several moving parts.

In some instances the retailer may prefer to use an existing store display fixture in order to promote certain merchandise. To help the store operator customize such a display, some manufacturers provide product "decorating kits." These kits usually contain shelf-trimming materials, price cards, and signs. All of this material is intended to increase sales by promoting product image and attracting the target market. Be careful, however, in using point-of-purchase decorating kit materials. Because there are no standard sizes for various display fixtures, kit materials may not fit or attach properly to existing displays. A cluttered and unattractive display unit can be the result. Good planning, careful fixture selection, and careful placement of the kit materials can help avoid such problems.

Shelf Management System

Air Space System

Frame-Out System

Boutique System

Illustration 36 The four types of point-of-purchase design systems are shown here: shelf management, frame-out, air space, and boutique.

SUMMARY

Point-of-purchase displays are a specialized form of visual merchandising planned to reach customers who are in the store and who will buy. Retailers want point-of-purchase displays that will get the customer's attention, identify the product and provide information about it, and motivate the customer to buy. While point-of-purchase displays can have specific promotional functions, ultimately they are judged on how well they sell products. Point-of-purchase units are of several types and may be found at any location in a store. Wherever they are located, their purpose is to get the customer's attention and encourage a decision to buy. Some point-of-purchase display materials are given to retailers by suppliers or vendors. In other cases, point-of-purchase visual merchandising is a planned feature of the store design and is developed and maintained by store staff through the use of commercially available fixtures.

6. ADVERTISING DISPLAYS AND EXHIBITS

The purpose of this section and related projects is to help students:

- Distinguish among three types of exhibits.
- Develop questions to be asked in considering possible use of advertising displays or exhibits.
- Follow an organized procedure in planning exhibits.
- Develop a design for an exhibit or advertising display.
- Set up an exhibit in a manner consistent with the purpose and product(s) featured.
- Become acquainted with materials and installation techniques in exhibit displays.
- Understand how to apply exhibit techniques to in-store visual merchandising.

The primary objective of point-of-purchase display presentations is to stimulate immediate sales. However, there are other forms of display that are designed to be primarily informational. These displays often are called institutional displays and the most common forms are *advertising displays* and *exhibits*. These displays stress the quality of the product and the image and integrity of the business. They provide information about the value and use of a product. The major users of advertising displays and exhibits are manufacturers, vendors, and other suppliers of goods and services to industrial and consumer markets. Exhibits are used by businesses that have periodic opportunities to "show off" their products at trade shows, vendor and retailer conferences, and other events that cater to potential buyers of their goods. Advertising displays are used when manufacturers or agencies want their firm or product featured in public places such as airports, convention centers, or shopping malls. These visual presentations attempt to pack a lot of information into a limited space. In addition, advertising displays and exhibits usually incorporate the best of modern visual technology and design into their presentations. Thus, these forms of display and the techniques they use are often an ideal answer to the presentation needs of retailers, particularly service businesses such as hair care shops, business service suppliers, and banking and financial institutions. A knowledge of advertising and exhibit displays can be valuable to a display person, even to one intending to do store displays. The focus of this section will be on the creation of exhibits.

TYPES OF EXHIBITS

Most exhibits by individual business firms can be included in one of the following three categories: permanent, portable, or single-event. Each of these may be staffed or unstaffed, that is, they may have one or more persons at the exhibit to talk with interested viewers or they may consist simply of the display.

Permanent Exhibits

Permanent unstaffed displays are found in locations where there is heavy public traffic. Shopping malls, major hotels, convention centers, and airport terminals are good locations. These displays may range from wall-mounted posters or photographs to elaborate settings featuring actual products. New cars, boats, campers, mobile homes, and farm equipment may be on open display. Smaller products may be enclosed in cases or placed on turntables where they are visible to the public, but out of reach.

Permanant exhibits that are usually staffed can be found in wholesale markets or convention centers. The Merchandise Mart of Chicago and the Dallas Market Center are examples of large facilities with permanent exhibits. Products on display include furniture, appliances, apparel, textiles, housewares, art, and carpets. Buyers from retail establishments can examine a wide range of goods in a relatively short time by visiting such market centers.

Illustration 37 Exhibits are found in public places, trade shows, and merchandising marts. Some exhibit firms are organized to provide exhibits and exhibiting equipment to other businesses.

Portable Exhibits

Portable exhibits are designed to be used for a period of time in one location and then dismantled and sent on to another location. Exhibitors arrange to place their displays in a location for a few weeks or during a particular event. For example, a major manufacturer of glassware prepares five new portable exhibits every year. These exhibits then are scheduled to be used in various parts of the country at events where the company feels its products should be featured. The exhibits may be staffed by local sales representatives.

Single-Event Exhibits

For some manufacturers there may be a single annual event of such importance that they will develop an exhibit just for one use. For example, a household appliance manufacturer may prepare an exhibit of new products for just one annual showing at the Housewares Exhibition at McCormick Place in Chicago. Such a single-event exhibit usually is designed to highlight or introduce new merchandise or a new line of products. Because of this, a company's exhibit probably will be redesigned each year. Single-event exhibits usually are staffed by some of the top company representatives.

PURPOSE OF EXHIBITS

The most frequently given reasons for firms to participate in exhibiting are to increase, maintain, or recover what they consider their share of a market. Other reasons are to promote a new trade name, introduce a new product, or show a new application of an existing product. For many firms, exhibiting is their main means of keeping in contact with customers and of staying up to date on trade developments and competition.

When should a firm get involved with exhibits? This is a fundamental question that must be answered carefully. Just because beautiful exhibits can be created does not mean exhibits should be used. Answers to the following questions will give a business firm some indication of whether or not it should consider exhibits:

1. Is the use of exhibits suitable for our type of business or product?
2. Would a program of exhibiting serve to reach our desired market(s)?
3. Do we have good opportunities to exhibit within our market area?
4. Would exhibiting complement our present promotional efforts?
5. Are the costs of exhibiting within the scope of our promotional budget?
6. Do we have access to expert help in planning and creating exhibits?

The answers to some of these questions will be more significant than others. From a hard-nosed business point of view, the matter of potential market contact with a meaningful number of customers is highly important. If a business firm is planning to introduce a new product, buying exhibit space and presenting an exhibit might be a wise decision if that event attracts a large number of potential buyers. If the event does not attract potential buyers, there is little reason to sponsor an exhibit.

The use of exhibits is not limited just to manufacturers and large corporations. Smaller firms may find that local business shows and merchandise fairs can be profitable. Locally sponsored events such as farm and home shows may be ideal exhibit opportunities for small and independent businesses. For example, a small dry-cleaning firm rented space at a local show and demonstrated its rug-cleaning service. As a result of this two-and-a-half-day show, the owner of the firm obtained enough orders for rug cleaning to keep the firm's staff busy for nearly three months.

Illustration 38   Exhibiting is an expensive means of promotion. Before deciding to use exhibits, business management should consider the purposes and values of exhibits for their company.

PLANNING AN EXHIBIT

Once a decision has been made to use an exhibit as a promotional tool, the next step is to plan the exhibit. The exhibit may be planned and developed by the firm's display staff or may be contracted for with outside consultants and free-lance display persons. In either case, the business staff will need to consider a great many questions before considering any possible designs. Some of the questions for which you will need answers are in the list that follows. Some of these questions will be considered in the process of deciding whether or not to use an exhibit; others will be faced for the first time during the planning phase.

1. What products will the exhibit feature?
2. Who will the exhibit visitors be?
3. What will be the primary interest of the visitors?
4. How long and under what conditions will each visitor be at the exhibit?
5. What supporting materials or personnel will be used?

6. What requirements as to the size and shape of the exhibit will be made by the location or exhibit management?
7. Will the exhibit be permanent or portable?
8. What is likely to be the nature of other exhibits at this event?

Planning the exhibit design will be much easier if these questions are answered. Once these questions are answered, the planners can move on to some of the more specific details of exhibit design. One important outcome of the planning phase would be a fairly specific statement of the business goal to be achieved by this exhibit. This goal becomes the basis for evaluating the results of exhibiting.

EXHIBIT DESIGN

As with most visual promotional presentations, the initial design ideas for an exhibit should be developed as rough sketches. It is not uncommon for a designer or a design team to develop five

Illustration 39   The well-planned exhibit will attract visitors even when competing with hundreds of other exhibits at a trade or merchandise show.

or six rough sketches, each with a significantly different presentation concept. The evaluation of these preliminary sketches and the selection of the most feasible idea helps prevent false starts and disappointments. These preliminary sketches nearly always consider materials, colors, treatment of merchandise, and, of course, the principles of display.

Most industrial and consumer products can be shown just as they are—ready for use by potential buyers. These real products can be touched and possibly moved by the viewers. If they are mechanical or electronic, they can be shown in operation. Some products can be shown partially disassembled. Others can be shown only in their finished versions but can be supplemented by supporting visuals of their construction. An important design consideration is whether the exhibit will be viewed just from one direction or from several directions. Getting the product into the central role in an exhibit is the purpose of a good design.

The best designs usually are those that are simple and functional. The design should assure that the exhibit itself does not interfere with the customers' interest in your product. Sometimes a firm needs little more than an attractive backdrop and a covered table for an exhibit. Products can be arranged on a table with small risers and holders used to lift the goods from a flat position.

The selection of colors for exhibits follows the same principles as color selection for good window or interior display. Refer to the discussion in Section 2 to develop good color schemes, and always remember to keep the colors of your products in mind. Primary colors are popular for exhibits, especially blue with accents of silver or gold. If some part of the exhibit is to be draped, be sure that drape colors and other exhibit colors are compatible.

Enlarged photographs or sketches of your product, in use or in the manufacturing process, are often a good means of adding both an informational and a decorative touch to an exhibit. Take the case of a pottery manufacturer producing several dozen sizes and varieties of pottery and needing to display them effectively in a small exhibit space. The designer selected just three pieces for display and then placed exact-scale photos of the others on two rotating pillars, one on either side of the displayed pieces. The result was a showing of the complete line of pottery, all in six feet by five feet of space.

Many firms use an enlarged version of their trademark or **logotype** (business identification symbol) as part of their decorative backdrop. Whatever signs are used should contain only the essential wording, printed in clear, bold lettering or in the usual type style of the company name. Exhibit signs are often limited in size and shape by the exhibit organizers. Whenever possible, try to have a design that will place the company sign high enough that it can be seen from a distance. Also, try to use a many-sided sign that can be seen from several

Illustration 40 This exhibit features consumer goods—clothing—displayed on the backdrop and shown from the rack to store buyers.

Illustration 41 Here an industrial product—cable insulation for information systems—is featured in an exhibit which uses photos, brochures, and samples to inform viewers.

directions. Consider the various typical exhibit shapes shown in Figure 6-1 and determine what type of sign would be most effective for each.

While developing your design ideas, remember that customers will pick up exhibit literature containing detailed information about your products. The display can stress only the most important features and interesting facts. An attractive means of dispensing sales literature should be included in your exhibit design, so that you benefit from the extra promotional impact of a printed document containing additional information about your firm and your products.

The ideal exhibit design should provide a functional but artistic background and base for the merchandise or service presentation. The size, material, color, or lighting of the exhibit should never be permitted to overpower the products to be featured. A simple design, well planned, is likely to be more effective than a complex design that might be more costly and more difficult to build and install.

EXHIBIT CONSTRUCTION

Often the exhibit design will specify particular materials or fixtures to be used in the exhibit. In other cases the design may allow for a choice of materials in the construction of the exhibit. Whatever materials are used, they should be selected with regard for the merchandise to be featured. A chrome and glass structure might be appropriate for one exhibit, while for another softer materials, such as draping and acoustical panels, would be best. Sometimes a floor or table surface is needed for demonstration. Lighting, of course, is always a concern. Do you need overhead lighting? Do you need spot lighting? How do you get the appropriate lighting?

The range of materials that can be used in building an exhibit is extensive. As a visual merchandiser, you will need to choose the combination of materials that would be best for each exhibit. All the standard materials described in Section 8 should be considered. If the exhibit is to be portable, avoid using glass. Moving an exhibit in and out of show sites, lifting it into and out of trucks, and storing it from time to time can lead to broken glass and disappointment. When the effect of glass is necessary, consider using tempered glass or some of the excellent clear plastics that now are available.

When the exhibit structure is to be reused and transported from one location to another, the dismantling and reassembly must be made easy. Often this put-up and take-down operation will be carried

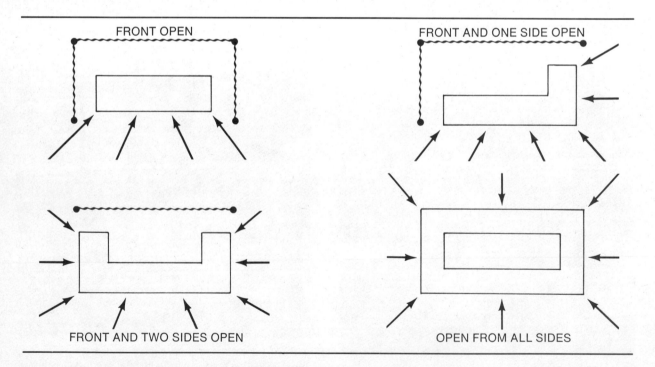

Figure 6-1 The diagrams above show four different exhibit shapes, with backgrounds indicated by wavy lines. The arrows show different possible approaches by viewers. It can be seen that the various angles of approach require consideration when exhibits are being designed.

Illustration 42   After design and materials have been determined, the exhibit can be built in the display shop.

out by people who have little skill or experience in such work. The procedure must be easy and uncomplicated. An exhibit structure that folds into a self-contained shipping case should be given several tests under working conditions before it is considered "show ready." A display structure that has bent hinges, splintered surfaces, or scratches and gouges as a result of repeated use will not make a good impression. As in the design of other displays, the selection of simple but substantial materials for exhibit construction often is the best choice.

EXHIBITING CONTRACTS

At many trade shows and exhibit sites there are several conditions that are imposed on the exhibitors. These specifications about the conditions under which the exhibit may be shown may be quite restrictive. When a firm decides to sign a contract for exhibit space, the details of that contract should be examined carefully. The following questions should be asked about any exhibit contract:

1. Does the contract allow you to use your own staff in preparing the exhibit in the area assigned?
2. Will you be able to use your own staff to move the exhibit structure and materials into and out of the exhibit building?
3. What is included in the contract — electrical service, backdrops, signs, chairs, tables?
4. Does the exhibit organizer provide security services?

5. What is the liability of the organizer for both property and personal damages?
6. Must the exhibit be installed and removed during a specific time period?
7. Will storage be provided if an exhibit arrives early or needs to be held after the exhibit period? Is there an extra charge for storage?
8. Is the space contracted for clearly marked and identified so no disputes will arise between exhibitors?

While many of these questions may seem very specific, only if they are answered can an exhibitor adequately prepare for installation of an exhibit. The additional charges for some of the services mentioned can really run up the cost of exhibiting. In fact, these additional costs and the loss of control over some aspects of the exhibit may cause a firm to decide not to exhibit. For these reasons it is important that the conditions of exhibiting be known in advance.

DISPLAYING EXHIBITS

When the decision to exhibit has been made, the exhibit planned, a design developed, materials selected, and the conditions of exhibiting clarified, then the visual presentation is put together. Products featured in an exhibit should be displayed in such a manner that they will have the greatest impact possible upon the exhibit visitor. Whenever possible, featured products should be available for personal examination by customers. If you are displaying small household appliances, set them up to perform just as they would in the home. If you are displaying microcomputers or software, your exhibit should encourage visitors to try the computers and run through some sample programs. When demonstrating the actual products is not practical, then showcases with goods or samples should be an important element in the exhibit. If the actual goods are too large for the exhibit, you might consider audiovisual presentations. Films, videotapes, or slides can provide visitors with an understanding of the product. Machinery shown with cutaway sections, shown partially disassembled, or shown with viewing ports into specially designed pieces will permit an "inside" look that will have high interest value for customers.

Where your product line consists of several different items, attempt to group similar items in one area of the exhibit. For instance, if you are featuring a line of hardware, try to group all the hand tools in one section, the power tools in another, and possibly the larger bench equipment in a third area.

Illustration 43   In this exhibit, the technological product itself is shown in use.

If possible, arrange to have the tools in use. A few pieces of wood, some nails, and two or three sample hammers will invite customers to try out various hammers by driving a few nails. Always try to show the product in use.

Exhibitors frequently, and mistakenly, attempt to crowd all their merchandise into one exhibit booth. The purpose of an exhibit usually is to feature just the newest and very best products a firm has to offer, so concentrate on showing only a representative sample.

High-quality work and cleanliness are essential in displaying an exhibit. One guideline is that the exhibit should be at least as good as the best display a firm would have in its own business place. People who attend many exhibits are keen critics. They form early judgments about a firm on the basis of what they see, that is, the quality of the exhibit and the manner in which it is maintained. If your exhibit looks shoddy, visitors will assume that your products also are shoddy.

The arrangement of the exhibit, the way it is displayed, the product promotion involved, and the use of printed material for distribution to customers will depend to some degree on whether the exhibit is staffed. If the exhibit design includes the idea that a person or persons will meet and assist visitors, then some additional questions need to be considered. Will these staffers be trained to work on this exhibit? Do these staffers have responsibility for displaying the exhibit? To what extent do these staffers have in-depth technical and sales knowledge about the product?

Whenever possible, an exhibit should be staffed by the people who are most knowledgeable about the featured products. Perhaps this means that a team of engineers and marketers would make the best staff. Even when knowledgeable individuals are used, they should be briefed about the exhibit and how they might use it to the firm's best advantage.

The person who has overall responsibility for an exhibit should obtain **evaluation cards** from the staff, if staff are used, as well as **reaction cards** from the visitors who have stopped at the exhibit. Also, there should be a way to count how many people saw the exhibit, how many stopped for at least a brief time, how many visited with the exhibit staff, and how many customers purchased the product or asked for follow-up contact by the company.

SUMMARY

At this point you may feel overwhelmed about working with exhibits. While there are many different things to consider when planning a good exhibit, keep in mind that exhibits are just another form of visual merchandising. A good understanding of display principles, display design, and visual presentation will serve as the basis for work with exhibits. Remember that exhibits, just like displays, are expected to show products or ideas effectively to prospective buyers and to promote sales for the business.

7.   PLANNING VISUAL PRESENTATIONS

The purpose of this section and related projects is to help students:

- Understand the importance of planning in developing effective visual presentations.
- Recognize the impact of proper merchandise selection on the planning process.
- Use various store promotions and competition as resources when creating display themes.

- Recognize the value both of various visual merchandising publications and of their own personal files as sources of ideas for new visual presentations.
- Select themes and merchandise that blend well together.
- Describe the development and use of a display-planning calendar.
- Recognize the value of maintaining a display-planning budget and identify items that should be included in this planning tool.

Good displays do not just happen by chance! Most often they are the result of creativity, skill, and — most importantly — planning. Visual presentations usually are designed to sell merchandise or promote ideas. Therefore, the impressions they create must be favorable. Customers entering a store for the first time often do so because they have been impressed favorably by something in the merchant's window displays. Entering the store is one thing — making a purchase is another. That is where interior displays take over. If these visual presentations are well planned and well constructed, the chances are that the merchant will sell merchandise.

Besides attracting customers and promoting merchandise and ideas, visual presentations communicate an overall impression or image of the store. It is important for the display designer to know what the store's desired image is and to make sure that it is a part of every display. In order to create displays that can attract customers, sell merchandise, and create a good image, specific attention must be given to *display planning*.

The basis for good display planning is an idea that is simple and can be identified easily. Potential customers constantly are exposed to television, newspaper, magazine, and billboard advertisements. As a result, they expect to see displays that are attractive, attention getting, and to the point. To accomplish these things, a presentation has to be planned thoughtfully. Techniques that can

prove helpful in planning visual display presentations are discussed in this section.

SELECTING MERCHANDISE

The first step in successful display planning is to choose the merchandise to be presented. Few

Illustration 44   A display setting and theme can be designed to project a particular store image. Here quality and exclusiveness are emphasized.

effective display designs are created when merchandise is selected after the plan for a presentation has been formalized. Displays that contain unrelated items of merchandise result in customer confusion and do not attract attention. Always keep in mind that displays exist to serve merchandise; merchandise is not meant to serve displays.

SELECTING A THEME

Every visual presentation starts with an idea, or **theme**. Sometimes that idea can be difficult to *identify*. This is particularly true when one believes that the only source of ideas is the person whose job it is to design the display. In actual practice, most displays result from creative combinations of bits and pieces of many display design ideas. If you are able to come up with an entirely new display idea—great! But for most visual presentation designers, this rarely happens. Therefore, in order to begin planning displays, you need to be aware of possible sources for display ideas.

Merchandise

Merchandise selected for display often provides clues as to how it can be presented. A product's major use can suggest an arrangement to show that use. Cookware on a stove, hats and scarves in a fall setting, even lawnmowers and hedge trimmers in a yard, are just a few examples of how a

Illustration 46 Here is an example of a lifelike product-in-use window display used by a sporting goods store to feature an exercycle.

product's use can be shown. What an item is made of and how it is constructed also can provide valuable clues for display ideas. Even the color, size, and shape of products can prove helpful. The possibilities are unlimited.

Store Promotions

Among the most valuable sources of display ideas are those which reflect seasons, holidays, special activities, or other store-wide promotions. Because most events of this type are held on a regular basis, care must be taken not to repeat the same display ideas too often. Sometimes the slightest change in a special-event display may be enough to keep it fresh. However, do not make changes purely for the sake of change. If the basic display idea still is effective for a particular event, use it again.

Other popular display themes are based on such things as color, price, process, or fabric. You are probably familiar with promotions built around

Illustration 45 Related items of merchandise, presented as they might be used, make a simple, effective display.

Illustration 47 Store-promotion displays are particularly effective in attracting a wide range of potential customers into a store. Sales promotions and special holiday promotions can have especially wide appeal.

themes such as White Sale (color), Crazy Day Sale (price), Spage Age Wizardry (process), or Wash and Wear (fabric). Though these familiar examples have been successful, do not assume that you should limit display planning to the most commonly used ideas. Visual presentation themes can be as varied as your imagination allows.

Competition

A leisurely stroll down the main street of a town or through a local shopping center can prove to be a surprisingly good source of ideas for visual presentations. If you try this means of gathering ideas, keep in mind the following suggestions: Decide which displays do the best job of holding your attention. Then try to determine *why* those particular displays are so effective. Write down any special design techniques you see, especially if they could be used in your own display projects. Always be ready to make written notes of what you see. Do not make the mistake of looking only at displays containing merchandise similar to that which you intend to use. You may, in fact, get some of your best ideas from displays containing completely different merchandise. It is entirely possible for a well-designed sporting goods arrangement to spark the idea needed to design an attractive reading lamp display.

Certainly display personnel in other retail stores can be excellent sources of new ideas. Do not pass up an opportunity to "talk shop." Remember, too, that display people always are seeking new ideas and will welcome the chance to talk with other display personnel.

Customers

One of the most obvious, yet often overlooked, sources of display ideas can be your own customers. Simply observe customer reaction to current displays. To some extent, you can measure display effectiveness by the number of customers who stop, look, and buy.

Sometimes it pays to ask customers what they think of a certain display. If you have created a display that is a "show stopper," find out *why* it works. Ask questions specific enough that customers' answers will be useful to you. Of course, you must be willing to accept criticism. Since most people are not familiar with the basics of display design, you must keep this limitation in mind while evaluating their comments. Your job is to translate customer comments into meaningful display design ideas.

Publications

The main offices of most retail chains regularly provide pictures of current display ideas for each of their stores. In addition, trade publications, such as *Visual Merchandising*, picture a variety of excellent merchandise displays in every issue. Sometimes product manufacturers make available examples of displays designed for their own products. It is also possible to find ideas for merchandise displays in newspapers, in magazines, and on television.

Personal Files

Collect and keep a file of all the good display ideas you can find. Cut out pictures, take notes, and write down ideas. Take photographs of displays, especially your own most successful displays. This file will serve as a ready reference, saving you a great deal of time and effort in planning future visual presentations.

THEMES AND MERCHANDISE MIX

How a display theme or idea finally is chosen is not as important as how well it works in motivating customers to buy the merchandise being presented. Most successful display designers believe that a single-theme display is much more effective than a display with several themes. Displaying merchandise not related to the central theme often confuses the customer and cuts the selling power of the display. For example, a display on the theme of "Fall Adventures" probably would not be very effective if swimsuits on sale were shown near fall coats and winter jackets. Placement of closely related items makes the theme more believable and increases the display's effectiveness. Also, a sign that communicates the theme at a glance promotes understanding and increases sales.

If, for any reason, it should be necessary to place unrelated merchandise in a single display unit, grouping the most closely related items could help. Consider using several small signs to identify "mini" themes in the display. Where there is a choice, however, avoid mixing unrelated merchandise and using multiple-theme displays.

SKETCHING DISPLAY DESIGNS

Once the merchandise for display has been chosen and a display idea or theme determined, then the design for the display must be created. Several rough sketches of the proposed design should be completed. Putting ideas on paper before constructing the display will save time and will result in a more effective display. Sketches do not have to be artistic or detailed. In fact, a few lines or shapes representing the items to be used in the display should be sufficient. Time also can be saved by including a list of the materials and tools needed to complete the visual presentation. From these basic drawings it should be possible to choose the design most likely to have the greatest sales appeal.

Principles and Elements

The proper use of the various elements and principles of display in the planning stage is very important. Making sketches will help you plan the correct use of specific elements and principles. Sketches also make it possible to judge whether or not merchandise lines, shapes, sizes, textures, weights, and colors fit well together. In addition, sketching will help you to determine whether or not the display design has proper harmony, contrast, emphasis, balance, and proportion.

Signs and Props

The placement of showcards and signs will be worked out from your sketches. Such printed items can then be prepared in advance to speed up final display construction. Display props needed to raise, form, or drape merchandise, or to carry out a theme also can be determined in advance. Because displays often are constructed within a specific time frame, it is also important to make sure that required props will be available and in good condition.

If there is any question regarding the value of sketching a display layout before the display is built, the sketch's worth will be proven when the display is started. Now all preplanned elements can be brought together, and construction of the display will go more smoothly. The disorganized, last-minute hustle and frustration resulting from forgotten details and poor planning will be avoided.

LONG-RANGE DISPLAY-PLANNING TOOLS

The amount of time spent in planning visual presentations should be kept to a minimum. There are two important techniques which can be used to make display design and construction easier and more effective. These are the display-planning calendar and the display-planning budget. The *display-planning calendar* is a record of all the visual presentations to be built during the coming year. The *display-planning budget* is a list of expected costs in designing and constructing each display. The more information each planning record contains, the more effective future display decisions will be. Most retailers display merchandise throughout the entire year. Thus, display planning becomes a year-round job.

Display-Planning Calendar

There is no single display-planning calendar that can be used by all retail merchants. Stores vary in terms of merchandise sold, location, and management attitudes about long-range planning. Retailers must know what their own particular needs are. The display-planning needs of a small neighborhood hardware store, for example, would be different from those of a department store located in a large shopping center.

Illustration 48   The "before" and "after" of a well-planned visual presentation.

But whatever a store's specific needs are, some basic guidelines can be helpful in organizing a display-planning calendar. First, make a list of all regular merchandise-promotion events. (Perhaps the store has a Back-to-School Sale, a Manager's Sale, a Spring Sale, and other such promotions each year.) This list should be as complete as possible. Second, make a list of all holiday-related merchandise promotions. This list would include Christmas, Easter, the Fourth of July, Thanksgiving, and other holidays. Only those holidays for which displays are to be designed and constructed need to be considered. Third, consider any community or civic functions for which displays could be designed. These might include such things as school programs, sporting events, merchant association promotions, and service or social club activities. Fourth, list the expected new and specially priced merchandise from various suppliers. Finally, make a combined list, organized by date, of all the information shown on the individual lists. This final list is the skeleton of the display-planning calendar. The final calendar should contain not only the displays to be designed, but also the deadline for the completion of each display.

Display-Planning Budget

What actually can be done to create good displays depends in part on the funds available for that purpose. But large amounts of money spent on display work will not automatically guarantee good results. The key to successful display design is always the display person. Still, it makes good business sense to know (as closely as possible) how much it will cost to design and complete the displays called for in the planning calendar. It also will be to your advantage as a display planner to know in advance just how much money will be available for displays. Then changes can be made if necessary. Keep in mind that some retailers consider visual presentations to be an expense rather than an investment. Therefore, good sales results from a display could mean more money available for future displays.

Illustration 49   Planning displays that will attract attention and increase sales can be a creative and exciting time.

The following suggestions may prove helpful in identifying design expenses which should be included in the display-planning budget. List any special props or fixtures needed to complete each planned display. The purchase price of things such as special lighting, signs, draping materials, floor covering, or other accessories should be listed. The cost of special tools and basic supplies (paints, nails, wire, staples) also should be estimated.

Budget planning might even include the cost of any merchandise damaged or altered during display construction.

The overall plan (display-planning calendar and budget) tells when you may, or must, design displays and what resources you have to work with. Neither the size of the business nor the amount of display work to be done will change the need for planning. The results, in terms of more attractive and more effective displays, will be worth the effort.

SUMMARY

Most visual presentation specialists agree that successful displays result only from careful planning. Putting ideas on paper in advance of display construction can eliminate errors, save time, and increase the sales potential of the items being presented.

Good planning involves careful selection of display merchandise and the identification of a theme that will capture customer interest. Sources of ideas for effective presentations can be found in the display merchandise, store promotions, competition, customers, publications, and the display designer's own file of previous displays. Planning is formalized when a sketch of how the display should look is completed. Such sketches should include the theme and the merchandise to be used and should indicate how the principles and elements of display will be applied. Props, materials, and signs needed to complete the display also should be noted. Display planning is most effective when the display specialist is able to plan in advance. Display-planning calendars and budgets are effective tools in organizing visual presentation activities.

8. VISUAL MERCHANDISING MATERIALS AND TOOLS

The purpose of this section and related projects is to help students:

- Identify the various types of ready-made materials used in display construction.
- Identify various materials used in the custom construction of displays.
- Develop ideas on how to utilize common materials in a variety of displays.
- Develop a list of materials needed for construction of a specific display.
- Set up an efficient storage and inventory system for display materials.
- Describe the use of a variety of tools and equipment used in display construction.
- Follow good safety practices in display construction.

If you were to keep a record of the display fixtures and props used by a store in your community for a period of a year you undoubtedly would be impressed by the variety of items used. Also, you probably would be surprised at how many of the same items are used over and over. Even smaller businesses need a wide variety of props and fixtures for their display presentations over a period of a year. To give the impression of a fresh look, the display designer and workers need to make creative use of display materials. The imagination to use a broad range of materials to produce quality displays week after week and year after year is a talent display workers must have. Because few businesses have the funds to buy an entirely new set of materials for each display, recycling and rebuilding become major activities of the display department staff. The display worker must be able to visualize ways in which the desired image can be created from the materials on hand.

The raw material for visual presentations is practically unlimited. Some items, of course, must be purchased from vendors of display fixtures and equipment. Many more, however, can be created from common materials. For a few cents' worth of paint and a few minutes of time, a scrap piece of wire mesh, formed into a shape and sprayed with lacquer, can become a striking backdrop for towels, scarves, yard goods, or gloves. The common store gondola fixture, with a bit of construction magic, can become a riverboat or a castle. The challenge to you as a display worker is to select the best materials available for the display job at hand.

DISPLAY MATERIALS

A complete listing of display materials available is not possible. The annual buyer's guide of manufacturers and distributors of visual merchandising products provided by *Visual Merchandising and Store Design* magazine lists 1,100 firms. Each of these firms has a wide variety of items suitable for visual merchandising presentations. In addition to these items, you probably will use some materials no one ever thought of using in displays, simply because you are a creative person. In this book, the major ready-made items will be presented and the common construction materials will be described, so that you know the basics that will be available to you. Major resources for display materials can be found in some of the sources listed in the Selected References section of this book. Every display worker should develop a list of resources from which he or she can get needed display materials quickly.

Display materials can be placed in two groups. **Ready-made materials** include those materials ready for immediate use in a display setting. Such items are obtained from vendors or suppliers and do not need to go through the display shop for fabrication or finishing. After repeated use, however, it is likely that some ready-made items will need to be reconditioned. The other group includes raw materials used in the construction of items that are not readily available as ready-made items. These raw materials must be sawed, formed, painted, or *custom constructed* in other ways before they can be used in a given display. Materials in these two categories are described in the following paragraphs.

READY-MADE MATERIALS

Earlier, you were introduced to a variety of functional props and fixtures that are used to hold or support merchandise for display. Decorative props and materials added to a display to complete a visual impression also were presented. These ready-made materials frequently are advertised in visual merchandising magazines and catalogs. The most common categories of ready-made materials offered by manufacturers and distributors are fixtures, mannequins, rotating and animated devices, backgrounds, letters and signs, and decorative materials.

Fixtures

Items used to hold merchandise in a display setting can vary from a simple plastic cube to an elaborate replica of a space vehicle. Fixtures for window and interior displays need not always be special items. Many regular store fixtures often can be used for display purpose. The material of the fixtures must reflect the image you are trying to build for the business within the particular presentation. A glass and chrome fixture conveys a different impression than a fixture made of walnut wood and wrought iron. Every display department should have a variety of fixture items that will meet the image requirements of a wide range of displays.

Mannequins

Mannequins are the "human" figures in visual presentations. Often these figures are so lifelike that customers at first may mistake them for real people. Mannequins clearly are the main form of display material used in clothing displays. They are expensive, however. Often they are the most costly item in the display manager's budget. Modern techniques of mannequin manufacture are very exacting. Eye, skin, and hair color, cast of features, and posture can be provided to suit any business demand. The cost of full-form mannequins begins at about $400 and goes up, depending upon their style, quality, and detail. Because mannequins cost so much, their selection and care must be taken very seriously in display work.

Before you begin to search for mannequins, be sure of your needs. Some business firms selling clothing items have decided not to use mannequins, even though their merchandise suggests that mannequins could be used. If you do decide to use mannequins, then you need to determine how many of each type you really need to meet your display requirements. The types available include partial forms (torsos, legs, arms, hands, heads) and full forms (adult, child, female, male). Before buying any mannequins, think of the mannequin inventory you want to have five years from now. Only then can your selection be made in a sound manner.

Reconditioned mannequins are available at a considerable savings over the price of new ones. When new forms might be too expensive, a business should consider investing in reconditioned forms. The reconditioned mannequin will look like new, but its style will be that considered fashionable at the time it was manufactured.

Rotating and Animated Devices

Motion is an effective addition to many displays. **Turntables** and **ceiling rotators** are standard pieces of equipment in most display departments. A rotating display is eye-catching and permits viewers to see the merchandise from all sides.

When selecting a turntable, think about the size and weight of merchandise that will be supported. Small turntables can support a few pounds, while larger tables can support items as heavy as an automobile. Rotators should have at least two speeds: 3 rpm (revolutions per minute) and 1 rpm. Faster rotators may have limitations — their speed may prevent customers from seeing the merchandise clearly. Most turntables and ceiling rotators operate with small electric motors, so electric power cords must be considered in their use. Sometimes the smaller sizes, particularly ceiling rotators carrying very lightweight items, may be powered with 1.5 or 9 volt batteries.

Many firms have established a tradition of using **animated displays** for certain holiday visual presentations. Skating rabbits, hard-working elves, dogs that move their heads and wag their tails, and dancing children are all products of imaginative display workers. Through the use of modern electronics, the art of display animation has grown rapidly, producing almost lifelike performances by mechanical figures.

Animated displays can be great crowd attractors. Such displays are expensive, but they may be well worth their cost. If display staff members cannot construct their own animated figures, such items may be purchased from display houses that

Illustration 50   Mannequins come both in almost-lifelike forms and in abstract forms. They are expensive props but add tremendously to the presentation of clothing items.

Illustration 51   Motion in a display can attract attention and even cause the customer to see the merchandise in a new way. This "swing" and lightweight cloth mannequin are kept in gentle motion by the natural air drafts near the store ceiling.

specialize in developing animated scenes. Some businesses may contract with such firms for a different set of animations every year. This plan saves the expense of in-store construction or of repairing and storing items each year.

Backgrounds

Many visual presentations need a full or partial background to create the proper setting. Backgrounds may be made with sheets of rigid material such as paneling, mirrors, glass, wood, or plastic. Backgrounds also may be made of flexible material such as fabric, paper, or other drapable material. Paper backgrounds can present preprinted scenes, photo murals, or textured surfaces.

A background should contribute to the display setting—not dominate or distract from the mer-

Illustration 52   Animated displays can become part of community events and are especially attractive to younger customers. This eye-catching display of plastic dinnerware and picnic items uses a toy airplane with a revolving propeller.

chandise being featured. A good test of a background is whether or not the viewer notices it for itself alone. A good background simply should enhance the merchandise on display, perhaps by establishing a realistic setting, or by establishing a sense of quality.

Letters and Signs

A supply of ready-made letters in various sizes and styles is essential in any display department. Because so many styles are available, the display manager should decide which letter styles will be used, then build a collection within the styles selected. Styrofoam, plastic, paper, wood, and metal have been used to create letters in every imaginable style and size. Classic, block, or script styles are used most often. While other styles may be used from time to time, it is best to have a good assortment of sizes in one or two of the most frequently used styles.

Illustration 53 Individual letters can be used in a variety of ways that will both tell and sell. An inventory of letters is an essential part of a display department's supply of ready-made materials.

Printed signs for displays often need to be created individually. These signs should be made with the same attention to size and style that is given to the selection of ready-made letters. The ability to use a *sign-making machine* should be one of the basic skills of every display worker. The growing use of microcomputers to create signs soon may make the use of these character generators a required skill also. Printed signs should be sharp, clear, and professional-looking. The colors of the sign should blend with or complement the color scheme of the display. Again, letter style is important. The style of letters used in printed signs usually should match the style of individually lettered messages. In the display, printed signs may be freestanding or mounted in sign holders.

Decorative Materials

The ultimate touch in many displays is a carved duck, a potted plant, an art piece, or some other item that reinforces the theme of the visual presentation. These items, which decorate a display but do not hold or support the merchandise being shown, are selected to provide realism and attractiveness. They add considerably to the desired effect of many displays.

As with backgrounds, the decorative materials should not dominate the display or detract from its main purpose—to show the merchandise. Most decorative materials are added to a display to give a sense of realism to the setting. Such decorative touches as grass for a display of golf shoes, a spray of cherry blossom for spring clothing, and sand and sea shells for beach wear, are important in creating the theme or seasonal image needed for the display. Items of merchandise to be used as props often can be borrowed from other departments in the store. You could use stuffed animals with children's clothing, towels and white goods with household appliances, tools or hardware with work clothes, or books with furniture. Such items serve as self-advertising displays as well as adding to the original visual presentation.

One caution about decorative materials and props—do not use them unless they are necessary

Illustration 54 A large stuffed toy contrasts with the children's bedding being featured and gives the display an attention-getting quality.

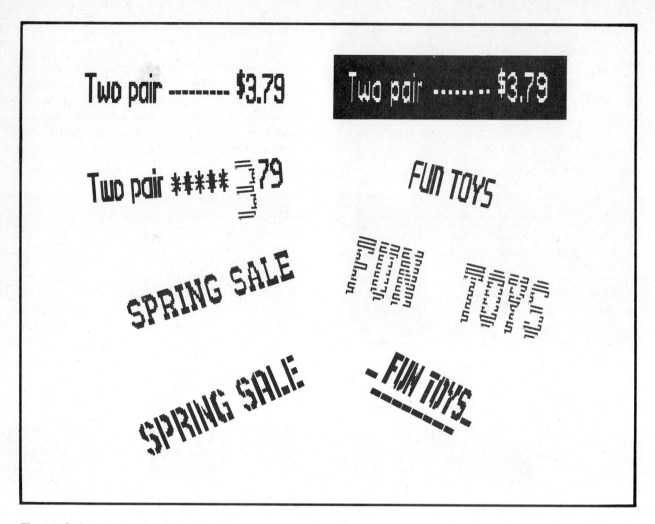

Figure 8-1 Microcomputer word generators can make available a wide variety of typefaces. The sign maker can try out several arrangements in just seconds and select the one best suited to a display.

to your design. Many excellent displays are created with only minimal decorative accessories. If you have any doubt about the use of decorative materials, first try the display without them. If the desired image can be achieved without the decoration, leave it out. "Simple is better" is a good motto to keep in mind in decorating a display.

CUSTOM-CONSTRUCTION MATERIALS

Often the particular item needed for a display cannot be found among the ready-made materials. This is not unusual, and when this situation occurs the item must be *custom constructed*. Most display workers accept the fact that frequently they will need to construct props, backdrops, or other items

needed for a display. There are many suppliers who specialize in providing materials specially designed or suited for construction of display items. With imagination, the display worker often can combine materials and make an outstanding display. Some of the materials most commonly used are described in the following paragraphs.

Dimensional Lumber

Lumber that is precut to standard sizes is referred to by its dimensions. The expressions "two by two," "two by four," and "one by six" refer to so-called standard sizes of lumber. The actual dimensions are different from these sizes. Thus a "two by two" is actually 1 1/2 by 1 1/2 inches, a "two by four" is actually 1 1/2 by 3 1/2 inches, and a "one by six" is 3/4 by 5 1/2 inches. Lengths may

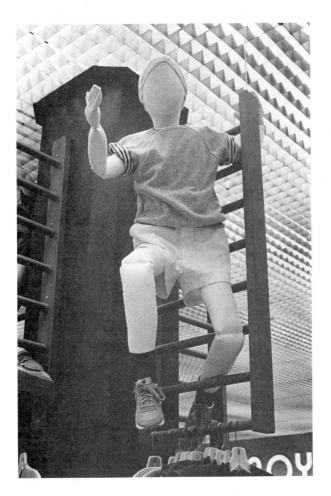

Illustration 55 Custom construction of display pieces can give visual presentations a very special touch.

vary but usually they are in multiples of 2 feet, starting at 8 feet and going to 24 feet or more in some dimensions.

Dimensional lumber comes in different grades. **Select** lumber is free from knotholes or imperfections. Select lumber is used where appearance is important. **Common** lumber has noticeable defects but is adequate for general-purpose construction. It is also less expensive than select-grade lumber.

Panels

Sheeting made from a wide range of materials is bought in panels. Some panels are designed for strength, others for lightness, others for ease in shaping into objects. Some have decorative surfaces. Panels come in varying thicknesses, widths, and lengths. Most wood-product panels come in widths of 4 feet and lengths of 8 feet, although some may be as long as 10 or even 12 feet. The most common panel materials are as follows:

PLYWOOD

Plywood is made from an odd number of thin sheets of wood, glued face to face with the grain of alternate sheets running at right angles. It generally comes in thicknesses of 1/4 to 1 inch. A variety of textures and finishes also is available. Plywood can be sawed and shaped just like solid wood.

HARDBOARD

Panels of **hardboard** are produced from softwood pulp made into sheets under pressure and heat. Hardboard may be tempered (treated with resins) and thus made harder and moisture resistant. Untreated hardboard is less expensive and is quite satisfactory for dry interior work where little strength is needed. Usual thicknesses are 1/8 and 1/4 inch. Hardboard may have a prepainted or a plastic-laminated surface, or it may be perforated. The perforated variety is referred to as **pegboard**.

PLASTERBOARD

Plasterboard has a core of gypsum and outside surfaces of heavy-duty paper. The paper face can be smooth or finished in various patterns. Plasterboard, or gypsum board, is inexpensive and fireproof and can be painted or papered. If this material is to be reused, treat it carefully. It is soft, and nail holes or dents show very readily.

FOAM CORE

Foam core panels are made like a sandwich, with the outside surfaces of wood veneer or coated paper and the core of lightweight plastic foam. These panels can be cut into a variety of shapes. They are easily sawed, require little sanding, and can be painted, silk-screened, flocked, or covered with fabric. Foam core panels are made in thicknesses up to 1 inch and have surprising strength for their light weight. They are fast becoming a standard item in the display workshop.

ACRYLIC

Acrylic is a rigid plastic which can be cut, drilled, and sawed with slow-speed power tools. An acrylic sheet can be bent by carefully heating the area of the bend and then forming it over a wood frame. Pieces of acrylic can be fastened together with glue, bolts, or metal clamps. The sheets come in a broad range of colors. Thicknesses from

1/32 inch to 3/8 inch are most common, but thicker sheets also are available.

Paper

Many paper products have been made especially for display work. Large sheets of paper work well for covering space or serving as a backdrop. Some papers are especially designed to accept lettering. An interesting use of paper is a **breakthrough**. In this design objects or merchandise appear to have broken through a paper background into the display area.

SEAMLESS PAPER

Seamless paper is a large-sized paper that comes in rolls up to 50 feet long and up to 107 inches wide. Because of the broad range of colors available, it can make an attractive large background surface. (Some suppliers also carry the paper 140 inches wide in white only.) Seamless paper can be decorated with art work, using paint or felt markers. Because it is seamless, it can be used in dramatic wall-to-wall or ceiling-to-floor coverings not possible with many other materials. It is easily cut, stapled, and tacked. The odd sizes and scraps may be cut into confetti pieces for colorful scatter on floor surfaces of a display.

TUBING

If you need a lamp post, a tree trunk, a Grecian column, or a common barrel, consider the use of **paper tubing.** Paper rolled into tubing is sold in diameters from 1 inch up to 30 inches and, in special cases, even larger. Paper tubing is light in weight, easily cut, has good weight-supporting quality, and can be painted or surfaced with a multitude of materials. In addition to the traditional round tubing made of paper products, circular and rectangular tubing is available in materials such as plastic, metal, or polyester fiber. The display workshop always should keep a variety of tubing sizes and lengths on hand.

CORRUGATED PAPER

Corrugated paper has parallel grooves and ridges that give the paper strength and flexibility, making it a long-time favorite in the display shop. Corrugated paper is usually 48 inches wide, comes in rolls up to 25 feet long, and has a color or preprinted design on one side. It can be rolled, cut, and shaped into a variety of display props.

Illustration 56 Paper backgrounds can be used in a variety of ways to set the stage and/or theme for a display.

SPECIAL PAPERS

In addition to the papers already mentioned, there are papers with velour, foil, and many other textures. These provide the display worker with a broad range of options for display. Some papers are treated so that paint will not soak through or spread (bleed). Other papers are treated so that they will not reflect light or create a glare that would detract from the display setting. Papers with special qualities can provide that extra touch when a particular setting is desired. Crepe paper is an example. It is a lightweight paper with a crinkled surface. Crepe paper can be shaped by stretching. It is available in rolls 20 inches wide by 100 feet long and 48 inches wide by 25 feet long, or in streamers (rolls) 1 7/8 inches wide and up to 500 feet long.

Fabrics

Fabrics made from natural or synthetic fibers, in various weaves and designs, serve exceptionally well for display drapery and backgrounds. In cases where a feeling of elegance is desired, fabrics usually serve better than paper products. The most commonly used display fabrics are taffeta, felt, velvet, and burlap. Taffeta is used where crispness or luster is needed. Felt, an unwoven fabric, has little tensile strength and no stretch, but it can be cut or formed into various shapes and will not ravel. The term "velvet" covers a variety of fabrics that are woven face to face and cut apart while still on the loom. Velvet material is used where a plush or formal display setting is desired, as in displays of jewelry, fine china, silver, and glassware. Burlap is a coarse woven fabric which gives a rustic or primitive tone to a display. Fabrics can add a touch of distinction, but recent display practice shows that use of them is declining except in smaller displays.

MATERIAL INVENTORY AND STORAGE

In addition to a supply of the items already mentioned, there are always many miscellaneous items around the display department. It does not take too long for the display staff to collect a supply of cinder blocks, chains, barrels, and similar items obtained from friends, flea markets, and garage sales. In order for the display department to be kept in good order, some inventory and storage system must be maintained. If the display staff is to know what material is available, a system of organization is necessary. When something is needed, it is a waste of time to search through shelves and closets and a waste of money to buy something you already have.

Display managers have found that a coding system is helpful for inventory and storage. Assign to every useful display item a letter and number. An inventory sheet will show both the letter and number for each item, with the letter indicating the storage area. It is always a good idea to tag display props and fixtures with the date they were used in a presentation. Such date tags on items will indicate if they are used frequently enough to make keeping them worthwhile. Needed but infrequently used items can be stored separately from those used regularly.

Whatever system of inventory is used, items placed in storage should be protected from damage and dust. In particular, mannequins need to be enclosed in covers to protect them from dust and moisture. They also need to be placed where they will not be bumped or scratched by other items.

Display items represent a sizeable investment, and with proper care they can last for many years.

DISPLAY DEPARTMENT TOOLS

A variety of tools is essential for any display department. If the department does any custom construction work, it will use both hand and power tools. As in any good shop, these tools must be kept in good condition and returned to racks or tool cases when not in use. The basic categories of tools used by display workers are hand tools, power tools, fastening tools and adhesives, and painting tools.

Hand Tools

A good collection of hand tools is needed by any display department. For those departments that do custom construction, additional hand tools are needed. A basic set of tools includes hammers, screwdrivers, open and box-end wrenches, drills, squares, hand saws (both for wood and for metal), clamps, and a variety of pliers. A person who wants to go into display work but is unfamiliar with the use of these tools should take a course in the care and use of basic hand tools.

Power Tools

Band saws, saber saws, sanders, and ***routers*** are standard power tools used for cutting, shaping,

Illustration 57   A well-arranged shop with good tools is a necessary part of an active and productive display department.

and forming the variety of materials used in display construction. These power tools can be used to cut out letters, logos, and decorative shapes from wood, plastic, plasterboard, foam, light metal, and similar materials.

Power tools make work easier but can cause injury when used carelessly. Instruction in the proper use of these tools is essential to assure safety. These tools should be used only by trained persons or by persons working under the close supervision of experienced workers. Power tools must be checked periodically for wear, and worn or faulty electrical cords and connections must be repaired promptly.

Fastening Tools and Adhesives

Fastening materials together is a necessary, and sometimes frustrating, part of display work. Display workers use a variety of devices to make materials stay where they are placed. Two of the most common devices are staples and adhesives.

Choice of staple and staple length will depend upon the fastening to be done. Remember that every staple used will have to be removed. Many display workers prefer to use *T-shaped staples* instead of the more common U-shaped staples. T-staples are especially useful in fastening fabrics and delicate paper installations.

Your choice of adhesives should be based on the materials to be fastened. The common white glues in squeeze bottles that are used around the home and in schools (PVA adhesives) are suitable for use in interior displays. They form strong bonds but take only modest stress and do not withstand dampness. *Contact cements* are useful for plastics, hardboard, some foams, metal, and wood. Work must be laid out carefully in advance, because most of the bonding strength of contact cement is reached immediately when the cemented surfaces are pressed together. *Epoxy adhesives* are two-part adhesives. Made of a resin and a hardener, they will join almost anything, but they are more expensive than other adhesives. They are excellent for metal-to-metal and glass-to-glass bonds. *Electric glue guns* are used where an on-the-spot adhesive is needed. These glue guns use solid *glue sticks* which, when heated, turn to liquid. This type of adhesive is quick-drying and provides a reasonably strong bond.

Painting Tools

Display painting is done with brush, sponge, roller, or spray. Brush painting most often is used for smaller painting jobs or where careful artwork is necessary. When larger surfaces must be painted, roller or spray application frequently is used. Spray painting is well suited for large areas and for areas where pressure from a roller or brush cannot be applied. For small jobs, or when a special paint is needed, paint in spray cans may be sufficient. All painting tools, especially spray equipment, should be cleaned thoroughly after each use.

SAFETY IN DISPLAY CONSTRUCTION

Safety First! No amount of haste ever excuses an injury to oneself or another person. Display work requires the use of tools and equipment which carry the possibility of injury with them. Make it a regular practice to observe the safety rules for all of your work.

Wear safety goggles whenever you are working with materials that may splinter or fly through the air. Use the right tool for the right job — do not use a screwdriver for a hammer or a chisel for a pry. Whenever paints and painting equipment are being used, the area should be well ventilated and painters should wear masks to avoid breathing in paint or vapors. A type B fire extinguisher should be within reach. Of course no open flame should be allowed in the painting area. Proper ventilation also is important in the use of some adhesives, and contact of adhesives with skin always should be avoided. Exercise care in working with electrical cords and connections in order to avoid shock.

When working on displays in public areas, be sure to curtain or barricade the space so that people will not be injured. It is a good idea to do as much construction work as possible in the display shop first. There you have the best control over the use of materials. If work is necessary at the display site, it should be done, whenever possible, at a time when customers or others are not present.

Before opening a display to public view, make sure that no one can be injured by it. There should be no objects that might cut or snag viewers. Be sure that props, fixtures, and merchandise are securely fastened. Then unexpected pressure will not collapse display material onto a viewer. On open displays, think especially about any potential danger to children. Youngsters frequently approach and deal with a display in a manner quite different from that of adults. "Childproof" every display.

Each year, fires are caused by the combustion of display materials placed too close to lights. Such fires may result in injury to people and extensive

Illustration 58   Display workers always should use safety equipment when working with power tools.

damage to the business involved. Check each display to be sure that fabric and other flammable materials are not placed next to heat-producing lights or heat ducts, or in positions where sunlight through glass might cause fire. Be sure to have the correct types of fire extinguishers nearby. Become familiar with the heat tolerances of all common display materials and check each new material selected.

RESOURCES

Many items needed for display projects can be obtained from store fixture companies and local building and hardware dealers. The major source of needed items, however, will be the manufacturers and distributors that specialize in visual merchandising and display materials. Catalogs from these firms will serve as ready references for thousands of display items and materials. Names of resource firms as well as great display ideas can be obtained from a magazine such as *Visual Merchandising and Store Design* and from the trade journals for your business specialty.

Extensive showings of display materials and ideas can be found at the Visual Merchandising Center and the Merchandise Display Association showrooms, both in New York. The annual California Merchandising Show is sponsored by the Western Association of Visual Merchandising. The National Association of Display Industries sponsors shows in many major cities. These shows, plus the regular showrooms of wholesalers and manufacturers, offer a wide variety of display equipment and materials.

In addition to these associations, there are a number of professional groups that relate to the display industry. Examples include the Institute of Store Planners, the National Association of Store Fixture Manufacturers, the Point of Purchase Advertising Institute, and the Exhibit Designers and Producers Association. Depending on the work that you do, membership in a related association or professional group can be very beneficial. In addition to gaining new ideas, you can meet and become personally acquainted with many other people engaged in display.

Display work is dynamic; it never stands still. It offers a constant challenge to creativity and to merchandising skills. Certainly display work is a career in which it is important to grasp opportunities for sharing work experiences with others.

SUMMARY

The difference between a so-so display and a "customer stopper" often depends on the materials used and the quality of construction. The display worker needs to know what materials are available, both those ready-made and those for use in custom construction. In addition to knowing these materials, the display worker must know how to use tools to create and construct displays. Safety in display work means following correct procedures and checking and rechecking displays to assure that accident possibilities are eliminated. Display materials and ideas are available from many sources, but primarily from manufacturers and distributors of specialized display materials.

SELECTED REFERENCES

Books

Barber, Bruce T. *Designer's Dictionary Two*. Cincinnati: Signs of the Times Publishing Company, 1981.

Coutchie, Mariann. *Jewelry on Display*. Cincinnati: Signs of the Times Publishing Company, 1982.

Mang, Karl, and Eva Mang. *New Shops: Fifty-Two International Examples of Design and Construction*. New York: Architectural Book Publishing Company, 1982.

Novak, Adolph. *Store Planning and Design*. New York: Lebhar-Friedman Books, 1981.

Pegler, Martin M. *Dictionary of Interior Design*. New York: Fairchild Books, 1982.

Pegler, Martin M., ed. *Store Windows That Sell, 1980-81*. New York: Retail Reporting Bureau, 1980.

Pegler, Martin M. *Stores of the Year: A Pictorial Report on Store Interiors 1979-80*. New York: Retail Reporting Bureau, 1979.

Pegler, Martin M., ed. *Store Windows That Sell*. Vol. II. New York: Retail Reporting Bureau, 1982.

Pegler, Martin M., ed. *Visual Merchandising and Display*. New York: Fairchild Books, 1983.

Strong, C. J. *Book of Designs*. Cincinnati: Signs of the Times Publishing Company, 1981.

Wohlwend, Franz. *The Best No. 2*. Atlanta: Inspiration Press Corporation, 1980.

Wood, Barry James. *Show Windows: Seventy-Five Years of the Art of Display*. New York: Congdon and Weed, 1982.

Magazines

Merchandising Power. New York: Point-of-Purchasing Advertising Institute.

Visual Merchandising and Store Design. Cincinnati: Signs of the Times Publishing Company.

SECTION 1

PROJECT 1

Name _____

Course _____

Date Assigned _____

Estimated Finish _____

Date Finished _____

Evaluation _____

INFORMATION ABOUT VISUAL MERCHANDISING

To learn about and then keep up to date in the exciting field of visual merchandising, you need to have information from several sources. These sources of information can be books, articles, films, pictures, and photo slides. In this project you will locate various informational sources on the subject of visual merchandising that are available to you in your school and community. When you have finished this project, you should have a fairly good list of magazines, books, films, picture files, and slides that provide information about visual merchandising. You will want to add additional sources as you study other sections of this text and as you obtain experience in visual merchandising work.

In the spaces provided below and on the reverse side of this sheet, fill in the blank spaces, telling where each of the sources you have found is located (school library, instructional materials center, community library, classroom, instructor's office). Also, write a short statement about what the source contains. Some typical references and sample statements are given. Use other sheets of paper as necessary for each category. Try to make your list as complete as possible.

Magazine	Where Is It?	What Does It Contain?
Visual Merchandising and Store Design	School library	Articles and ideas on visual merchandising, display, and store planning. Many ads for display equipment and materials.

Book	Where Is It?	What Does It Contain?
Fundamentals of Merchandise Presentation. Robert Colborne	Classroom reference shelf	Overview of visual merchandising and its relationship to other merchandise functions. Covers department specialty stores. Many illustrations.

Films and Slides	Where Is It?	What Does It Contain?
Display slide collection	Instructor's office	35 mm color slides of interior and window displays taken at Strawberry Mall (prepared by last year's VM class).

SECTION 1

PROJECT 2

Name _____

Course _____

Date Assigned _____

Estimated Finish _____

Date Finished _____

Evaluation _____

VIEWERS' EXPECTATIONS OF VISUAL PRESENTATIONS

Business firms use visual presentations to provide viewers with an opportunity to see products that the firm has for sale. Visual presentations or displays often show viewers how the merchandise might be appropriate for their use. However, customers sometimes expect different things from displays. Some want to see visual presentations that are attractive and creative. Others want displays that are entertaining to their children. Some displays will cause some people to stop and look but may not spark any interest in other passersby. In this project, you are to interview three persons on what they expect from a good visual presentation or display. Record the answers to the interview questions in the spaces provided, and then summarize what you have learned about customers' expectations of visual presentations.

Interview One:

What information would you like to get from a visual presentation? _____

_____

What type of visual presentation or display is most likely to cause you to stop and examine the product

being featured? _____

_____

What problems would you have if businesses did not display merchandise they have for sale? _____

_____

Interview Two:

What information would you like to get from a visual presentation? _____

_____

What type of visual presentation or display is most likely to cause you to stop and examine the product

being featured? _____

_____

What problems would you have if businesses did not display merchandise they have for sale? _____

_____

Interview Three:

What information would you like to get from a visual presentation? _____

_____

What type of visual presentation or display is most likely to cause you to stop and examine the product being

featured? _____

_____

What problems would you have if businesses did not display merchandise they have for sale? _____

_____

_____

Summary:

Based on the expectations of the persons you interviewed, what do you conclude regarding the information

viewers expect to get from visual presentations? _____

_____

_____

_____

Based on the responses of those interviewed, what type of presentation seems most likely to cause viewers

to stop and examine the product? Did all three interviewees respond in the same manner? _____

_____

_____

Based on the responses of those interviewed, how important do you think displays are in helping customers

in their buying? _____

_____

_____

_____

_____

_____

SECTION 1

PROJECT 3

Name _____

Course _____

Date Assigned _____

Estimated Finish _____

Date Finished _____

Evaluation _____

SELLING POWER OF VISUAL PRESENTATIONS

The primary purpose of a visual presentation or display is to sell the merchandise featured. The five steps of selling through visual presentations are much the same as the selling steps of advertising or personal selling. For this project, select two window displays, each from a different local business. Using the forms below and on the next page, evaluate each presentation. Be sure to explain your judgments fully.

Display One

Business: _____   **Location:** _____

Describe the window display: _____

_____

_____

_____

_____

_____

Attract Attention: Do you think this display can get the customer's attention?   ___ Yes ___ No

How, or why not? _____

Arouse Interest: Do you think this display can arouse the interest of viewers?   ___ Yes ___ No

How, or why not? _____

Create Desire: Does this display clearly present advantages of the merchandise?   ___ Yes ___ No

How, or why not? _____

Build Confidence: Do you think this display builds confidence in the merchandise?   ___ Yes ___ No

How, or why not? _____

Direct Action: Does this display encourage the viewer to take action?   ___ Yes ___ No

How, or why not? _____

Display Two

Business: _____   **Location:** _____

Describe the window display: _____

_____

_____

_____

_____

_____

Attract Attention: Do you think this display can get the customer's attention?   ___ Yes ___ No

How, or why not? _____

Arouse Interest: Do you think this display can arouse the interest of viewers?   ___ Yes ___ No

How, or why not? _____

Create Desire: Does this display clearly present advantages of the merchandise?   ___ Yes ___ No

How, or why not? _____

Build Confidence: Do you think this display builds confidence in the merchandise?   ___ Yes ___ No

How, or why not? _____

Direct Action: Does this display encourage the viewer to take action?   ___ Yes ___ No

How, or why not? _____

Describe how each of the displays you evaluated might be improved in terms of its selling power.

Display One: _____

_____

_____

_____

Display Two: _____

_____

_____

_____

SECTION 1

PROJECT 4

Name _____

Course _____

Date Assigned _____

Estimated Finish _____

Date Finished _____

Evaluation _____

WORKERS IN VISUAL MERCHANDISING

Visual merchandising covers a broad range of work, but the most common employment is in store display work. The five most common job titles in store display work are (1) display director or manager, (2) display specialist, (3) display assistant, (4) trimmer, and (5) free-lance specialist. In this project you are asked to obtain specific information about the job requirements for persons who have these job titles. Use a variety of sources — such as want ads, position descriptions, display literature, library books, and interviews with business people — to obtain the information needed. Under "Job Description" indicate what the worker does, what tasks he or she performs. Under "Educational Requirements" indicate what education the person should have for the job. Under "Prior Experience" indicate what work experience employers usually expect. Under "Salary Range" indicate the typical salaries per week or per month. Under "Work Environment" indicate the working hours, where the person works, and the conditions of the work location (alone or with others, noisy or quiet, indoors or outdoors, clean or dirty).

DISPLAY DIRECTOR (Give specific job title) _____

Job Description: _____

_____

Educational Requirements: _____

Prior Experience Desired: _____

Salary Range: _____

Working Environment: _____

DISPLAY SPECIALIST (Give specific job title) _____

Job Description: _____

_____

Educational Requirements: _____

Prior Experience Desired: _____

Salary Range: _____

Working Environment: _____

DISPLAY ASSISTANT (Give specific job title) _____

Job Description: _____

_____

Educational Requirements: _____

Prior Experience Desired: _____

Salary Range: _____

Working Environment: _____

TRIMMER (Give specific job title) _____

Job Description: _____

_____

Educational Requirements: _____

Prior Experience Desired: _____

Salary Range: _____

Working Environment: _____

FREE-LANCE SPECIALIST (Give specific job title) _____

Job Description: _____

_____

Educational Requirements: _____

Prior Experience Desired: _____

Salary Range: _____

Working Environment: _____

Additional Comments

_____

_____

_____

_____

SECTION 2

PROJECT 5

Name _____

Course _____

Date Assigned _____

Estimated Finish _____

Date Finished _____

Evaluation _____

ELEMENTS OF DISPLAY DESIGN

In order to design displays that sell merchandise, a display person must have three kinds of knowledge: knowledge of the merchandise to be promoted, knowledge of the market to be served, and knowledge of basic display concepts. Display, or visual merchandising, is a planned combination of selected merchandise and display concepts intended to make a successful appeal to potential customers. This project reviews elements of display design. When used with merchandise and display units, these elements can create feelings of direction, movement, and mood.

In the sketch below, there are a number of line, shape, size, texture, and weight elements. (Color is presented in another project). Each element is lettered. Examine the sketch carefully, referring to the material in Section 2 under **Elements of Visual Merchandising Design.** Then answer the questions on page 84.

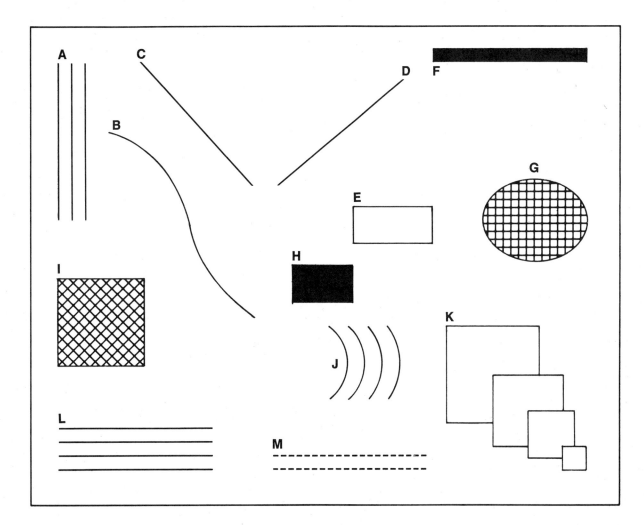

Items from the sketch may be used more than once in answers, and some questions may be answered with more than one letter.

1. Which item(s) represents texture? _____

2. Which item(s) gives the impression of quiet and calm, or width? _____

3. Which item(s) gives the impression of action? _____

4. Which item(s) gives the impression of rigidity, stiffness, and control? _____

5. Which item(s) gives the impression of flowing movement? _____

6. Which item(s) gives the impression of size? _____

7. Which item(s) gives the feeling of weight? _____

8. Which item(s) gives the feeling of poise, balance, dignity, or height? _____

In each of the spaces below, draw a line, shape, or other element to illustrate the word below each space.

Action	Dignity	Weight

Texture	Flowing Movement	Calm

SECTION 2

PROJECT 6

Name _____

Course _____

Date Assigned _____

Estimated Finish _____

Date Finished _____

Evaluation _____

USING COLOR IN DISPLAY

Each object in a display possesses some degree of color. Color, with its value and intensity, affects the amount of customer attention each object receives. Color, when properly used, greatly influences the potential customer's buying decisions.

Colors used in display can be classified according to color schemes. Basic schemes are those using complementary colors, split complementary colors, double split complementary colors, analogous (adjacent) colors, triadic colors, and monochromatic colors. It is extremely important that colors which "go well together" are selected for every display. Although basic color-scheme terms may sound confusing at first, this project will help you to understand them and to gain some practice in identifying each one.

Refer to this illustration when selecting display colors. To make the color wheel more useful to you, obtain a set of colored pencils and fill in the color circles.

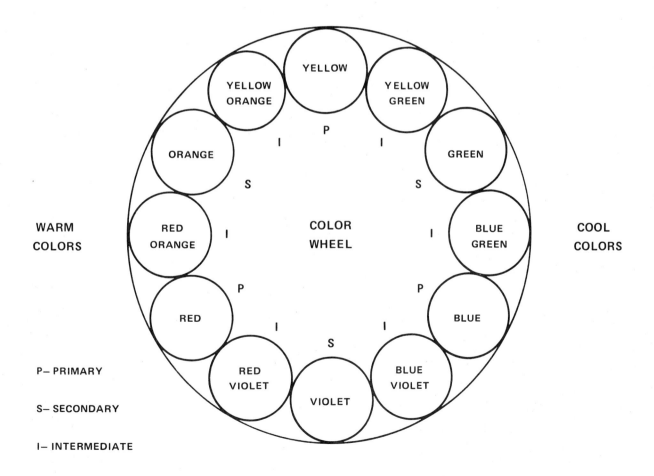

Complementary Colors are those colors directly opposite each other on a color wheel. The complement of a primary is always a secondary, and vice versa. Using the two blank circles, draw lines to show the complements of orange and of violet.

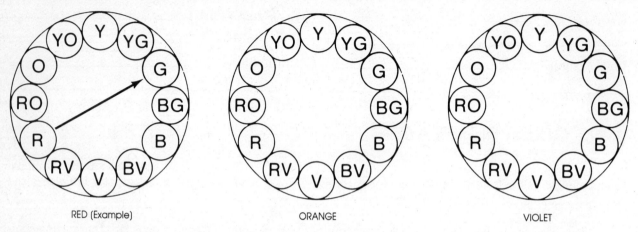

RED (Example)   ORANGE   VIOLET

Split Complementary Colors involve three points on the color wheel. The split complements of a color are the colors on each side of its complement. Using the two blank circles, indicate the split complementary colors of blue and of yellow.

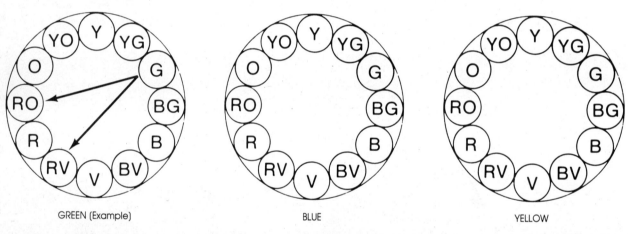

GREEN (Example)   BLUE   YELLOW

Double Split Complementary Colors involve four points on the color wheel. A color's double split complements are its two neighboring colors and the two neighboring colors of its complement. Show in the two blank circles the double split complements of yellow and of red orange.

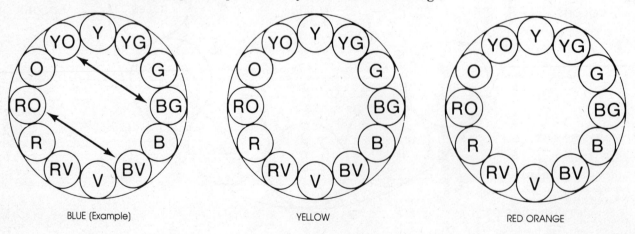

BLUE (Example)   YELLOW   RED ORANGE

Analogous Color schemes are made of any two or more adjacent (side by side) colors on the color wheel. A display may use as many as five analogous colors. Use of three colors is more common. For example, the three-color analogous color schemes for RED include (1) red orange, red, red violet; (2) orange, red orange, red; (3) red, red violet, violet. Refer to your color chart in answering the following questions:

1. What three-color analogous color schemes can be made using green? _____

   _____

2. What three-color analogous color schemes can be made using violet? _____

   _____

3. How many three-color analogous color schemes are there in a color wheel? _____

   _____

Triadic Color schemes are those that use the three colors at the points of an equal-sided triangle on the color wheel. One example is a scheme using the colors red, blue, and yellow.

1. What would be the triadic color scheme using violet? _____

2. What would be the triadic color scheme using yellow orange? _____

3. What would be the triadic color scheme using blue violet? _____

4. How many triadic color schemes are there in a color wheel? _____

Monochromatic schemes use one color in combination with different tints and/or shades of that same color. White and black are used in this combination. White can be added to a color until the color is a "tint" of almost pure white. Likewise, black can be added to a color until the color is "shaded" almost to black. For instance, when white is added to red, tints of pink (lighter red) are obtained.

1. What colors are obtained if black is added to red? _____

   _____

2. What colors are obtained if white is added to yellow? _____

   _____

3. What colors are obtained if black is added to yellow? _____

   _____

Now that you are familiar with color schemes, you should be able to select merchandise colors that can be used together effectively in a display. When you use complementary colors, remember that you are attempting to provide sharp contrast to draw the eye to the merchandise. To do this harmoniously, use small areas of a bright, intense color with relatively larger areas of weaker, lower value, opposite colors.

For each of the following merchandise items, indicate other appropriate merchandise and colors that could be used to give the item emphasis.

1. **Blue Scarves**	Merchandise _____	
	Complementary Color _____	
2. **Yellow Sport Shirts**	Merchandise _____	
	Complementary Color _____	
3. **Green Bedspreads**	Merchandise _____	
	Split Compl. Colors _____	
4. **Orange Sweaters**	Merchandise _____	
	Split Compl. Colors _____	
5. **Red Shoes**	Merchandise _____	
	Double Split Compl. Colors _____	
6. **Red-Orange Dishes**	Merchandise _____	
	Double Split Compl. Colors _____	
7. **Blue-Green Bath Towels**	Merchandise _____	
	Triadic Colors _____	
8. **Yellow Curtains**	Merchandise _____	
	Triadic Colors _____	
9. **Blue Coats**	Merchandise _____	
	Monochromatic Colors _____	
10. **Violet Dresses**	Merchandise _____	
	Analogous Colors _____	

SECTION 2

PROJECT 7

Name _____

Course _____

Date Assigned _____

Estimated Finish _____

Date Finished _____

Evaluation _____

PRINCIPLES OF DISPLAY DESIGN

The placement of merchandise in a display unit to create a desirable effect is directed by certain design principles. Knowing these principles will aid you in planning displays and will contribute to good display-building techniques. Basic arrangement of the elements of design into patterns is accomplished by using the principles of harmony, contrast, emphasis, balance, and proportion. This project will check your understanding of each of these design principles. You also will receive some practice in making basic display designs.

In the sketch below, there are several arrangements organized according to one or more of the display design principles. Examine the sketch carefully, referring to the material in Section 2 under **Principles of Visual Merchandising Design.** Then answer the questions on page 90.

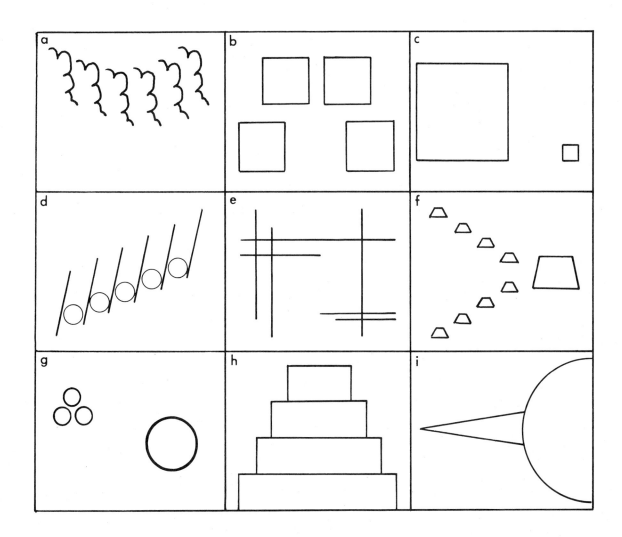

Items from the sketch may be used more than once as answers. Some questions may be answered with more than one letter.

1. Which item(s) illustrates the principle of harmony? _____

2. Which item(s) illustrates the principle of contrast? _____

3. Which item(s) represents the principle of emphasis? _____

4. Which item(s) represents the principle of balance? _____

5. Which item(s) represents the principle of formal balance? _____

6. Which item(s) represents the principle of informal balance? _____

7. Which item(s) appears to be out of proportion? _____

In each of the following spaces, draw a series of lines, shapes, or other elements of your choice to illustrate the display design principle named below the space.

Proportion   **Contrast**   **Harmony**

Balance in display is achieved by making each side of the display area equal in terms of size, shape, optical weight, color, and merchandise placement. Formal balance is achieved by making each half of the display identical with the other half in terms of the above qualities. Informal balance is achieved by optical equality: the components of each half of the display area may differ in terms of size, shape, optical weight, color, and number, but placement of the components is such that the display appears balanced. For informal balance, the heavier items are usually placed nearer the center, and the lighter or smaller items are placed farther from the center. Below are examples of formal and informal display layouts. Note that in each a dotted line indicates the center of the display unit area.

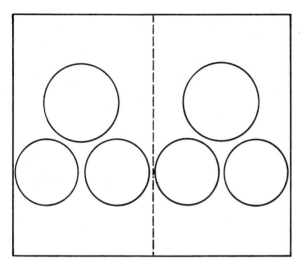

Formal Balance

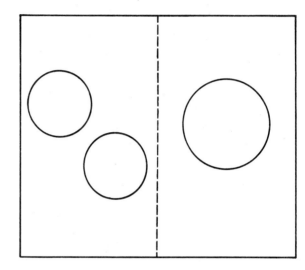

Informal Balance

On the spaces below and on the next page, create illustrations of formal or informal balance. Use as objects the number and types of coins indicated below the spaces. When you have found the proper arrangement, draw around each coin to make a sketch of the arrangement.

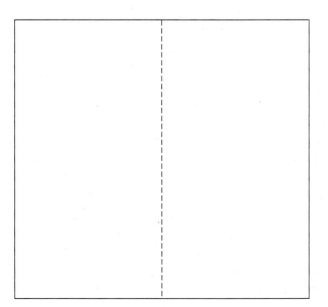

Formal Balance
(Five Dimes)

Informal Balance
(Two Dimes, Two Nickels, One Quarter)

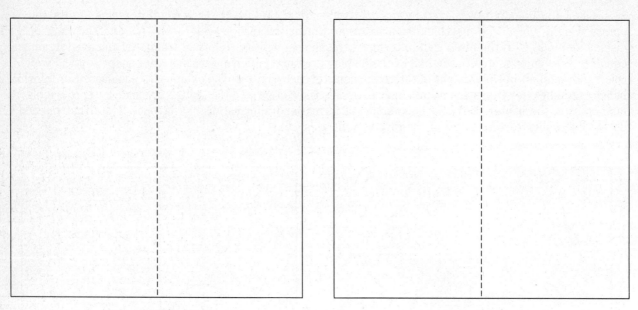

Formal Balance
(Four Pennies, Two Nickels)

Informal Balance
(Two Pennies, One Dime, Three Nickels)

Using the shapes at the left, sketch in the space provided a layout illustrating either formal or informal balance. Use all the shapes shown, and write below the space whether you are using formal or informal balance.

SECTION 2

PROJECT 8

Name _____

Course _____

Date Assigned _____

Estimated Finish _____

Date Finished _____

Evaluation _____

BASIC DISPLAY ARRANGEMENTS

Among the most commonly used arrangements in display work are the repetition, step, zigzag, pyramid, and radiation arrangements. These arrangements are described and illustrated below and on the next page. In the space beside each description, sketch a display which uses the arrangement described. Use merchandise with shapes that are easy to draw, such as cans, boxes, or cartons.

Repetition Arrangement. This is simple in form and achieves its effect through the repetition of similar items. Height, spacing, and direction are the same for all items. Some deviation is necessary to relieve the monotony. Such deviation can be achieved in other parts of the display through the use of panels and boxes, by placing some items at angles, and by using emphasis.

Step Arrangement. This is an informal arrangement and usually is effective as a side feature to a display. The difference in height from one level to the next should be the same, and all items should face in the same direction.

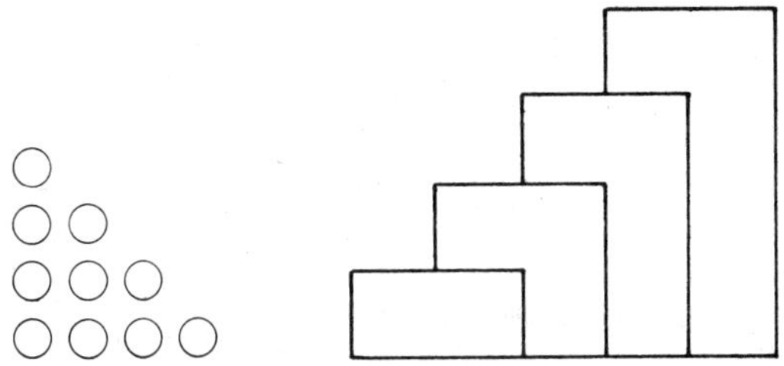

Zigzag Arrangement. The zigzag requires precise spacing to be effective. It is particularly adaptable to soft-goods displays where pedestals or stands of varying heights are used. Background or lighting may be used to highlight the zigzag and lead the eye through the total line.

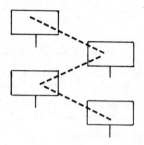

Pyramid Arrangement. The pyramid is a triangular arrangement culminating in a center peak made by the two sides converging. This is a formal arrangement and is effective with most merchandise. Small and large pyramids often are used together in a single display.

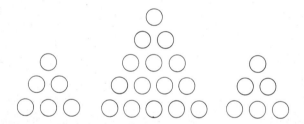

Radiation Arrangement. This formally balanced arrangement is an excellent way of placing emphasis on certain merchandise when other items are placed in the same display area. Display design elements such as shape, size, and color are important factors in the success of this arrangement.

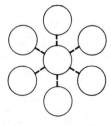

SECTION 2

PROJECT 9

Name _____

Course _____

Date Assigned _____

Estimated Finish _____

Date Finished _____

Evaluation _____

APPLYING DISPLAY CONCEPTS

Constant practice in the application of the various display concepts is absolutely necessary in order to develop solid visual merchandising skills. The purpose of this project is to provide you with an opportunity to apply those concepts using actual merchandise and available space. First, select several items of merchandise that have a related use. These items should be somewhat different in size, texture, and color. Next, identify a display unit, table top, or similar space that can accommodate the selected merchandise. If available, display materials and props also may be utilized. However, the intent of this project is to give you practice in demonstrating an understanding of the various display concepts discussed in Section 2 rather than practice in building a finished display. Complete the exercises below and on the next page.

Arrangement: Demonstrate your understanding of each of the basic display arrangements by placing your merchandise in appropriate positions to depict each arrangement. Then draw a general sketch of each completed arrangement in the space provided.

Repetition

Step

Zigzag

Pyramid

Radiation

Balance: Rearrange one of the displays shown on the previous page to demonstrate clearly the use of informal balance in merchandise placement. Sketch your new arrangement in the space below.

Color, Size, Texture: Choose a basic display arrangement and draw a preliminary sketch of a display that shows contrast in size, texture, and color in the merchandise.

Now arrange this display according to your sketch and have two other persons evaluate your arrangement to see if the contrasts you used are clearly visible.

Combining Display Concepts: Draw a sketch of a display that contains the merchandise you have been using in this project. Include as many of the basic concepts as will fit together appropriately in the display. Provide a summary giving reasons for your selection and placement of the display concepts.

Reasons: _____

_____

_____

SECTION 3

PROJECT 10

Name _____

Course _____

Date Assigned _____

Estimated Finish _____

Date Finished _____

Evaluation _____

IDENTIFYING WINDOW PRESENTATIONS

Window presentations may be classified by the type of unit in which they are placed, by the way in which the unit is used, or by the type of merchandise displayed. There are three basic types of window units: closed, semiclosed, and open. Standard uses of windows are for related merchandise items, for a line of goods, for a mass display, for some special event, and for sale displays. Refer to Section 3 for specific examples of each type of unit and for standard uses.

This project provides you with experience in identifying window presentations by unit design and use. You are asked to identify in your community a closed window, a semiclosed window, and an open window. In the spaces below and on the next page, describe each window unit, the display use, the merchandise, and the display idea or theme. Compare your analysis of each window with the analyses of other persons who have analyzed the same window.

Closed Window Unit

Business Firm and Location: _____

Description of Window: (size, placement in relation to entrance and to other windows) _____

_____

_____

Display Use: _____

_____

Merchandise Featured: _____

_____

_____

_____

Display Idea or Theme: _____

_____

_____

_____

Semiclosed Window Unit

Business Firm and Location: _____

Description of Window: (size, placement in relation to entrance and to other windows) _____

_____

_____

Display Use: _____

_____

Merchandise Featured: _____

_____

_____

_____

Display Idea or Theme: _____

_____

_____

Open Window Unit

Business Firm and Location: _____

Description of Window: (size, placement in relation to entrance and to other windows) _____

_____

_____

Display Use: _____

_____

Merchandise Featured: _____

_____

_____

_____

Display Idea or Theme: _____

_____

_____

SECTION 3

PROJECT 11

Name _____

Course _____

Date Assigned _____

Estimated Finish _____

Date Finished _____

Evaluation _____

WINDOW PRESENTATION COMPONENTS

Every window presentation contains certain components: (1) display background, (2) floor covering, (3) sides and ceilings, (4) merchandise, (5) props and fixtures, (6) lighting, and (7) signs. Different components are used in displays in different kinds of stores. For example, mannequins are display props often used for clothing and fabrics but rarely used in displays of hardware or appliances. Some components are parts of the window unit itself. Other components are items selected and arranged according to display concepts.

This project involves two activities. First, examine the display sketch below and identify the window presentation components shown. Record your description of each component under "Display #1" on the form on the other side of this page. Then select two displays in your community. Examine each display. Then report your descriptions of the components of these windows under "Display #2" and "Display #3" on the form on the other side of this page.

HIKING AND CAMPING EQUIPMENT

SECOND FLOOR

Window Display Components	Display #1 (Sketch)	Display #2 Store _____	Display #3 Store _____
Display Background (What is it?)			
Floor Covering (What material?)			
Sides and Ceiling (How are they treated?)			
Merchandise (What is featured?)			
Props and Fixtures (What are they?)			
Lighting (What kind is used?)			
Signs or Show Cards (What do they say?)			

SECTION 3

PROJECT 12

Name _____

Course _____

Date Assigned _____

Estimated Finish _____

Date Finished _____

Evaluation _____

MERCHANDISE SELECTION FOR DISPLAY

Merchandise placed on display is supposed to attract attention, arouse interest, create desire, build confidence, and motivate the potential customer to enter the store and take action. One way of discovering a display's ability to do those things is actually to observe the reactions of passersby to the display. What do passersby look at? Do they stop? Do they seem to look at just one merchandise item or one part of the display? Do they go into the store after looking at the display? A count of (1) the total number of people passing the window display, (2) the percentage of this total who look, stop, and examine the display, and (3) the percentage who enter the store will provide one measure of the display's success.

In this project you are to study the traffic flow past three different window displays. Make two copies of the Window Display Study Sheet on the next page, so that you have a total of three forms to fill out. Your purpose is to evaluate the power of the display and the merchandise to attract attention, to create interest, and (as much as possible) to create desire and induce action. Each window display and its viewers should be observed for a period of 20 minutes. Station yourself so that you can make an accurate count. Be sure that you do not interfere with traffic flow or entrance to the business. Record the required information on each of the three window display study sheets. The description of the merchandise should include its uses, color, sizes, styles, and any other characteristics. After your observation, calculate the percentages called for and answer the questions on the sheet. When you have completed all three window display study sheets, answer the following questions.

1. What merchandise seems to have the greatest appeal for the persons passing these three displays?

   _____

   _____

2. Did all passersby seem to be equally attracted to all three displays? If not, what differences did you observe?

   _____

3. Would day of the week or time of day have any bearing on the number of people who would be attracted to a display? Why or why not?

   _____

4. Would the merchandise appeal (sales, eye, time) be different for the merchandise in each of the three windows you observed? Explain your answer.

   _____

   _____

Window Display Study Sheet

Name of store _____ Address _____

Window display observed _____ **Number of windows in store** _____

Date of observation _____ from (time) _____ to _____

Description of display merchandise _____

_____

_____

_____

Traffic Count	Women	Men	Total	% of Total Traffic
Number of people *passing by* on sidewalk				xxxxxx
Number of people *looking at* display while passing by				
Number of people *stopping* to look at display				
Number of people *entering* store after looking at display				
Number of people entering store *without* looking at display				

1. Which merchandise appeal do you feel causes most viewers to stop and look at this display? (Choose one: sales appeal, eye appeal, time appeal).

    _____

    _____

2. To which item or part of the display do the viewers give most of their attention? _____

    _____

    _____

3. What merchandise do you feel could be changed or improved to make the window display more

    effective? _____

    _____

SECTION 3

PROJECT 13

Name _____

Course _____

Date Assigned _____

Estimated Finish _____

Date Finished _____

Evaluation _____

PLANNING WINDOW DISPLAYS

Careful planning of a window presentation is necessary if all the needed materials and merchandise are to be ready for installation on the appointed day and time. A missing prop or piece of merchandise can delay installation or even spoil a presentation that must be made without the needed item. Planning usually begins with an idea or a theme and then proceeds to selecting the merchandise, sketching the display, and listing the needed materials, including a showcard.

In this project, you are asked to develop three display planning sheets. The display idea for each is given, but you are to complete the rest of the plan. Use plain sheets of paper for the display sketch for each. Be sure that your list of materials (including lighting needs) is complete.

Display Planning Sheet #1

Display Idea: Women's shoes for spring and summer

Display Theme: _____

_____

Merchandise to Be Featured: _____

_____

_____

Show Card Copy (Wording): _____

_____

_____

Merchandise Needed	Props Needed	Fixtures and Materials Needed
_____	_____	_____
_____	_____	_____
_____	_____	_____
_____	_____	_____

Attach a display sketch drawn on a separate sheet of paper.

Display Planning Sheet #2

Display Idea: Mass display of summer sun-and-fun items (sunglasses, tanning oil, games, sand buckets, etc.)

Display Theme: _____

_____

Merchandise to Be Featured: _____

_____

Show Card Copy (Wording): _____

_____

_____

Merchandise Needed	Props Needed	Fixtures and Materials Needed
_____	_____	_____
_____	_____	_____
_____	_____	_____

Attach a display sketch drawn on a separate sheet of paper.

Display Planning Sheet #3

Display Idea: Men's casual slacks and jeans

Display Theme: _____

_____

Merchandise to Be Featured: _____

_____

Show Card Copy (Wording): _____

_____

_____

Merchandise Needed	Props Needed	Fixtures and Materials Needed
_____	_____	_____
_____	_____	_____
_____	_____	_____

Attach a display sketch drawn on a separate sheet of paper.

SECTION 3

PROJECT 14

Name _____

Course _____

Date Assigned _____

Estimated Finish _____

Date Finished _____

Evaluation _____

BUILDING WINDOW DISPLAYS

A window display should be installed quickly and with minimum disruption of customer traffic. Many firms install new displays during the hours that the firm is closed to customers or at times when customer traffic is light. To remove old displays and install new ones quickly, careful preparation of all display components must take place before actual installation. Since time is so valuable to the good display person, a routine or procedure should be established for planning, preparing, and placing the display components in the window. One time-saving technique is to use a checklist for major display items before placing them in the window. This check could be made by setting up the items in the display workroom area to make sure everything is on hand.

In this project, you are to plan and prepare two window displays featuring merchandise of your choice. Check with your instructor to see if you should do this project alone, with a partner, or with a team of classmates. The displays could be set up in a store, a classroom, a display laboratory, or a similar area that can provide appropriate display and viewing space. Be sure that the displays remain up until you have completed Project 15, which calls for an evaluation of one of the displays.

In the spaces below, summarize the essential features of each of the displays you build. On the reverse side of this sheet is a window display checklist that you should complete as you work on each display.

Display A

Display Theme: _____

Merchandise: _____

Basic Display Arrangement: _____

_____

Props to Be Used: _____

_____

Materials Needed: _____

_____

_____

Attach display sketch.

Attach show card copy.

Total time to plan and complete display: _____

Display B

Display Theme: _____

Merchandise: _____

Basic Display Arrangement: _____

_____

Props to Be Used: _____

_____

Materials Needed: _____

_____

_____

Attach display sketch.

Attach show card copy.

Total time to plan and complete display: _____

Checklist for Planning and Installing a Window Display

As you complete each step in the preparation of your displays, place a check mark in the proper column below. You may add to or change any of the steps listed to fit the routine you wish to follow. However, your routine must be complete.

	Display A	Display B
Planning		
1. Select main idea. Create theme for sign.		
2. List merchandise and materials needed.		
3. Make rough sketch.		
4. Write copy (wording) for show card.		
Window Preparation		
1. Return previously displayed merchandise to departments.		
2. Clean, repair, and store previously used fixtures and props.		
3. Remove floor covering and background and place in storage.		
4. Discard materials that cannot be used again.		
5. Clean entire display area.		
Display Preparation		
1. Assemble or order fixtures and props.		
2. Prepare background and floor-covering materials.		
3. Prepare the merchandise to be displayed.		
4. Make show card.		
5. Check on special lighting needs.		
6. Verify that interior displays and related advertising are ready (if coordinated).		
Execution		
1. Put in background and floor covering.		
2. Arrange fixtures and props.		
3. Arrange major and minor merchandise units.		
4. Put in accessories.		
5. Put in show cards and price cards (if used).		
6. Check lighting effects.		
Evaluation		
1. Note sales results from display (daily).		
2. Observe customer reaction to display.		
3. Obtain comments from department sales staff.		
4. Take a photo of display for idea file.		

SECTION 3

PROJECT 15

Name _____

Course _____

Date Assigned _____

Estimated Finish _____

Date Finished _____

Evaluation _____

EVALUATING WINDOW DISPLAYS

Viewing and evaluating displays is helpful in developing basic window presentation skills. Judging such factors as (1) the power to attract attention, (2) arrangement, (3) selling power, (4) timeliness, (5) lighting, and (6) quality of work increases your awareness of such factors when designing and constructing sales-building window presentations.

In this project, you are to evaluate one of the two displays you constructed in Project 14 and two displays you select from business firms in your community. Make two copies of the Display Rating Sheet on the next page, so that you have a total of three forms to fill out. Six major factors in judging window presentations are listed on the form, and several questions are given under each factor. These questions are to be used as guides in determining the rating each factor is to receive, but the questions are not to be individually scored. Rate each factor by checking a point somewhere on the scale. Checking "1" would indicate that you felt the display was weak on a particular factor. Checking "10" would indicate that the display was extremely strong on that factor. When all the factors have been rated, add up the point values of all the factors to obtain an overall score for the display. A perfect score is 60.

After evaluating and rating all three displays, answer the questions below.

1. Which of the displays had the greatest attention-getting power? _____ What made

   the attention-getting power of this display higher than that of the other two? _____

   _____

   _____

2. Which of the displays had the greatest selling power? _____ What made the selling

   power of this display higher than that of the other two? _____

   _____

3. Which of the displays made the best use of lighting? _____ Describe the lighting

   techniques used in this display. _____

   _____

4. Describe the ways in which the quality of the work in your display was better than or not as good as

   the quality of the work in the other two displays. _____

   _____

   _____

Display Rating Sheet

Name of Store and Display _____

Description _____ Total Points _____

Power to Attract Attention

Does the idea or theme have impact from a distance?
Is there an eye-catching use of color? of line? of motion?
Is there a powerful sign pointing out a special feature or price?
Is there human interest to arouse curiosity?

0   1   2   3   4   5   6   7   8   9   10

Arrangement

Is the merchandise made to look appealing?
Is the window, as a picture, attractive?
Is the design simple but the message strong?
Does the window design tell the quality level of the store?
Is the merchandise displayed as it might be used?

0   1   2   3   4   5   6   7   8   9   10

Selling Power

Are merchandise features clearly shown?
Is attention focused clearly on the merchandise?
Does the window's promise truly reflect the values in the store?
Does the theme help to arouse desire for the merchandise?

0   1   2   3   4   5   6   7   8   9   10

Timeliness

Is the merchandise well chosen for time appeal (season or event)?
Is the theme one with popular appeal at the time of the display?
Are the display colors appropriate to the season and merchandise?

0   1   2   3   4   5   6   7   8   9   10

Lighting

Does the lighting focus attention on the merchandise?
Is the lighting in good taste and not glaring?
Does the lighting strengthen the colors used in the display?
Is the lighting adequate for the window?

0   1   2   3   4   5   6   7   8   9   10

Quality of Work

Have interesting materials been used skillfully?
Is the lighting equipment expertly and safely installed?
Have the components been put together neatly?
Are all parts of the display clean and in good repair?

0   1   2   3   4   5   6   7   8   9   10

Comments: _____

_____

_____

SECTION 4

PROJECT 16

Name _____

Course _____

Date Assigned _____

Estimated Finish _____

Date Finished _____

Evaluation _____

INTERIOR DISPLAY PRESENTATIONS AND MERCHANDISE PROMOTION

Interior displays are part of a team that also includes advertising and window displays. All three work to gain attention, inform, and motivate. Potential customers usually become aware of a product by means of various advertising media. Window displays make it possible to show the actual items of merchandise that are being advertised. But it is the interior displays that bring customers into direct contact with the merchandise.

This project provides experience in (1) identifying and analyzing merchandise promotions that make use of advertising, window displays, and interior displays, and (2) planning a promotion using all three techniques.

1. Identify one product that is being promoted through advertising, window displays, and interior displays. Draw a brief sketch of each promotion and answer the questions below.

Product _____

What is being promoted? _____

_____

_____

Is the theme the same in all three promotions?

_____

_____

_____

Identify the theme(s). Does the wording vary in the three promotions? _____

_____

_____

_____

Does the merchandise vary in style, color, etc.?

_____

_____

_____

Is it clear that the three promotions are a coordinated effort to sell the same merchandise?

_____

_____

_____

Advertisement

Window Display

Interior Display

2. Select a product and provide rough sketches of your design ideas for each of the merchandise promotion techniques named below. Answer the question that follows.

Advertisement

Window Display

Interior Display

The purpose of each promotion technique is to sell merchandise. Briefly explain how you feel your

triple promotion idea will do this. _____

_____

_____

_____

SECTION 4

PROJECT 17

Name _____

Course _____

Date Assigned _____

Estimated Finish _____

Date Finished _____

Evaluation _____

INTERIOR DISPLAY DESIGNS

The ultimate success of any interior display depends on the design of the display unit, the location of the display, the fixtures used, and, most important, the merchandise being promoted. There are several basic kinds of interior display designs. These include: (1) open, (2) closed case, (3) island, (4) end, (5) platform, (6) shadow box, (7) background, and (8) point-of-purchase. Examples of each are given in Section 4.

This project asks you to visit several stores and locate what you consider to be one good example of each kind of interior display design. Record the information requested for each display in the spaces provided on this page and the following three pages.

Stores visited (after the name of each store, list the type of display seen there)

_____

_____

Open or Island Display

1. Where in the store was the display placed? _____

2. What merchandise was displayed? _____

3. What was the display's theme? _____

4. Do you think the display's primary purpose was to draw traffic or to increase sales? _____

_____

5. What other kinds of merchandise were nearby? _____

_____

6. Describe and evaluate this display using the following criteria:

   Power to attract attention: _____

   _____

   Merchandise arrangement: _____

   _____

   _____

   Selling power: _____

   _____

   _____

Closed-Case Display

1. Where in the store was the display placed? _____

2. What merchandise was displayed? _____

3. What was the display's theme? _____

4. Do you think the display's primary purpose was to draw traffic or to increase sales? _____

    _____

5. What other kinds of merchandise were nearby? _____

    _____

6. Describe and evaluate this display using the following criteria:

    Power to attract attention: _____

    _____

    Merchandise arrangement: _____

    _____

    Selling power: _____

    _____

    _____

End Display

1. Where in the store was the display placed? _____

2. What merchandise was displayed? _____

3. What was the display's theme? _____

4. Do you think the display's primary purpose was to draw traffic or to increase sales? _____

    _____

5. What other kinds of merchandise were nearby? _____

    _____

6. Describe and evaluate this display using the following criteria:

    Power to attract attention: _____

    _____

    Merchandise arrangement: _____

    _____

    Selling power: _____

    _____

    _____

Platform Display

1. Where in the store was the display placed? _____

2. What merchandise was displayed? _____

3. What was the display's theme? _____

4. Do you think the display's primary purpose was to draw traffic or to increase sales? _____

_____

5. What other kinds of merchandise were nearby? _____

_____

6. Describe and evaluate this display using the following criteria:

Power to attract attention: _____

_____

Merchandise arrangement: _____

_____

_____

Selling power: _____

_____

_____

Shadow Box Display

1. Where in the store was the display placed? _____

2. What merchandise was displayed? _____

3. What was the display's theme? _____

4. Do you think the display's primary purpose was to draw traffic or to increase sales? _____

_____

5. What other kinds of merchandise were nearby? _____

_____

6. Describe and evaluate this display using the following criteria:

Power to attract attention: _____

_____

Merchandise arrangement: _____

_____

_____

Selling power: _____

_____

_____

Interior Background Display

1. Where in the store was the display placed? _____

2. What merchandise was displayed? _____

3. What was the display's theme? _____

4. Do you think the display's primary purpose was to draw traffic or to increase sales? _____

   _____

5. What other kinds of merchandise were nearby? _____

   _____

6. Describe and evaluate this display using the following criteria:

   Power to attract attention: _____

   _____

   Merchandise arrangement: _____

   _____

   Selling power: _____

   _____

   _____

Point-of-Purchase Display

1. Where in the store was the display placed? _____

2. What merchandise was displayed? _____

3. What was the display's theme? _____

4. Do you think the display's primary purpose was to draw traffic or to increase sales? _____

   _____

5. What other kinds of merchandise were nearby? _____

   _____

6. Describe and evaluate this display using the following criteria:

   Power to attract attention: _____

   _____

   Merchandise arrangement: _____

   _____

   Selling power: _____

   _____

   _____

SECTION 4

PROJECT 18

Name _____

Course _____

Date Assigned _____

Estimated Finish _____

Date Finished _____

Evaluation _____

SELECTING AND LOCATING INTERIOR DISPLAYS

Interior display units must be matched properly with the display merchandise. Good matches result when (1) the interior display unit makes it possible to show the best features of the product, (2) attention is centered on the merchandise rather than on the display unit, and (3) where practical, the customer is able to directly inspect the merchandise being displayed. No matter how well the display unit and merchandise fit together, the interior display unit must be located where maximum sales will result. Suggestions for determining proper store location are found in Section 4.

This project provides an opportunity for you to match merchandise with display units and to choose an appropriate location for each display. For each merchandise item indicated below, give (1) your choice of an appropriate theme, (2) type of matching interior display unit, and (3) a specific location in a store in which you would place the interior display. On the following page, give the reasons for your choices.

Merchandise	Theme	Interior Display Unit	Location in Store
Tennis Shoes			
Charm Bracelets			
Backpacks			
Portable Stereo Tape Recorders			
Jogging Shorts			
Microwave Ovens			

Reasons for Choices

In the spaces provided, give a brief explanation of your choice of display unit and location for each of the types of merchandise.

Tennis Shoes   Display unit _____

_____

Location _____

_____

Charm Bracelets   Display unit _____

_____

Location _____

_____

Backpacks   Display unit _____

_____

Location _____

_____

**Portable Stereo
Tape Recorders**   Display unit _____

_____

Location _____

_____

Jogging Shorts   Display unit _____

_____

Location _____

_____

Microwave Ovens   Display unit _____

_____

Location _____

_____

SECTION 4

PROJECT 19

Name _____

Course _____

Date Assigned _____

Estimated Finish _____

Date Finished _____

Evaluation _____

BUILDING INTERIOR DISPLAY PRESENTATIONS

Interior displays, like window displays, should be installed or replaced quickly so as not to waste valuable selling space and time. Careful planning, along with a predetermined interior display installation routine, can make display building more efficient and result in increased sales of displayed merchandise.

Select two retailers who sell different lines of merchandise. Ask the persons in charge of display in both businesses to list the steps they follow in their interior display-building routines. Record the responses you receive in the appropriate spaces below. Use the Interior Display Routine Check Sheet on the next page as a guide in obtaining the information.

Retailer Number 1 _____

1. _____

2. _____

3. _____

4. _____

5. _____

6. _____

7. _____

8. _____

9. _____

10. _____

Retailer Number 2 _____

1. _____

2. _____

3. _____

4. _____

5. _____

6. _____

7. _____

8. _____

9. _____

10. _____

Prepare two interior displays using merchandise of your choice. Both displays may be located in a store, classroom, display laboratory, or similar area where appropriate display and viewing space is available. In this project you will carry out an activity dealing with the interior display-building routines of experienced display people. On page 118 you will find an interior display routine check sheet and on pages 119 and 120 you will find two planning sheets. All these will assist you in the completion of this project.

Interior Display Routine Check Sheet

As you complete each step in the preparation of the two interior displays, place a check mark in the proper column below. You may add to or change any of the steps listed to fit the routine you wish to follow. However, your routine must be complete.

Planning	Display 1	Display 2
1. Select main idea. Create theme for sign.		
2. List merchandise and materials needed.		
3. Select interior display unit.		
4. Select location in store.		
5. Make rough sketch.		
6. Write copy (wording) for show card.		
Area Preparation		
1. Return previously displayed merchandise to departments.		
2. Clean, repair, and store previously used fixtures and props.		
3. Remove floor covering and background and place in storage.		
4. Discard materials that cannot be used again.		
5. Clean entire display area.		
Display Preparation		
1. Assemble or order fixtures and props.		
2. Prepare background and floor covering materials.		
3. Prepare the merchandise to be displayed.		
4. Make show card.		
5. Check on special lighting needs.		
6. Verify that interior displays and related advertising are ready (if coordinated).		
Execution		
1. Put in background and floor covering.		
2. Arrange fixtures and props.		
3. Arrange major and minor merchandise units.		
4. Put in accessories.		
5. Put in show cards and price cards (if used).		
6. Check lighting effects.		
Evaluation		
1. Note sales results from display (daily).		
2. Observe customer reaction to display.		
3. Obtain comments from department sales staff.		
4. Take a photo of display for idea file.		

Interior Display Planning Sheet (Display #1)

Display Idea _____

_____

Display Theme for Sign _____

_____

Merchandise to Be Featured _____

_____

Interior Display Unit (Kind) _____

Location in Store _____

Show Card Copy (Wording) _____

_____

Materials Needed _____

_____

Display Sketch

Evaluate your completed display, using the questions on the Display Rating Sheet on page 108.

Interior Display Planning Sheet (Display #2)

Display Idea _____

_____

Display Theme for Sign _____

_____

Merchandise to Be Featured _____

_____

Interior Display Unit (Kind) _____

Location in Store _____

Show Card Copy (Wording) _____

_____

Materials Needed _____

_____

Display Sketch

Evaluate your completed display, using the questions on the Display Rating Sheet on page 108.

SECTION 4

PROJECT 20

Name _____

Course _____

Date Assigned _____

Estimated Finish _____

Date Finished _____

Evaluation _____

PINNING MERCHANDISE IN A VISUAL PRESENTATION

A currently popular display technique is the "pinning" of merchandise. The pinning of merchandise is accomplished by attaching items to be displayed to a flat surface, using straight pins. The pins are placed carefully so as not to be visible to the viewer. This method can eliminate the need for mannequins, body forms, and similar props in presenting soft line merchandise in interior displays. Pinning is particularly effective in making use of store space not normally used for display purposes.

Merchandise pinning is an action-oriented display technique. Its purpose is to present merchandise "in use." For example, slacks might be pinned so as to give the impression of walking or running. Shirts or sweaters might be arranged with the arms pinned in waving or swinging positions. Pinning is also effective in directing the viewer's line of vision to another product or to a show card in the display.

The following are some suggestions that prove helpful when pinning merchandise in an interior display: (1) start with a sketch of the desired layout; (2) place the merchandise in an action-oriented position on a flat surface, and attach the item with preliminary pins (ones that are visible); (3) adjust the product being pinned until the desired position is attained (correct in terms of bends in the elbows, knees, etc.); (4) place all permanent pins out of sight with heads away from the tension placed on the display item, and remove visible pins; (5) if more than one item is being displayed, overlap extensions such as arms and legs to save space; (6) avoid stretching the merchandise so tightly that the fabric looks unnatural; (7) apply the basic principles and elements of display in evaluating the pinning arrangement.

In the space provided below, draw a sketch of a display in which merchandise is pinned against the display background. Indicate how other related merchandise would be utilized to complete the display.

Display Sketch (Pinning)

Build the display sketched above and evaluate the results, using the questions on the Display Rating Sheet found on page 108.

SECTION 4

PROJECT 21

Name _____

Course _____

Date Assigned _____

Estimated Finish _____

Date Finished _____

Evaluation _____

FLYING MERCHANDISE IN A VISUAL PRESENTATION

A display technique called "flying merchandise" involves the suspension of a product in a display area by means of wire and nylon line. This technique makes it possible to utilize space for display that otherwise might go unused. Merchandise flying is a highly effective means of gaining customer attention because of the unique appearance that it creates. Like merchandise pinning, the flying technique is particularly effective when used with such soft line items as slacks, sweaters, skirts, pants, scarves, ties, etc. In each case the display item is presented "in action."

It is of particular importance to note that the suggestions (offered in the previous project) dealing with merchandise pinning apply equally to merchandise flying. In addition, it is recommended that soft wire be used inside the display item to give it a realistic shape and that the less visible nylon line be used outside the item to attach it to supports. Ceiling hooks, posts, and metal grids make excellent support "tie ups." Cup hooks or similar devices work equally well when no other means of tying up the display item are available.

In the space provided below, draw a sketch of a display in which flying merchandise is the major emphasis. Indicate, if applicable, how other related merchandise would be utilized to complete the display.

Display Sketch (Flying)

Build the display sketched above and evaluate the results, using the questions on the Display Rating Sheet found on page 108.

SECTION 4

PROJECT 22

Name _____

Estimated Finish _____

Course _____

Date Finished _____

Date Assigned _____

Evaluation _____

DESIGNING EFFECTIVE SHOW CARDS

The following suggestions should prove helpful in developing the skills necessary to create good show card copy.

How to Recognize a Good Show Card: A good show card is a silent salesperson. It increases sales by stopping customers to inform them of benefits offered by the merchandise. It also can present new fashions, ideas, and ways to make life better. A good show card can do a selling job for you by telling a sales story the customer otherwise cannot know. It answers customers' questions, assures them of values, suggests ways they might use the product, and encourages them to make purchases.

How to Write Effective Show Card Copy: When a customer glances at a show card, that fact shows that the customer is already interested in the merchandise. The show card must tell customers what they want to know about the product at a glance — what the product is, what it can do, and what it costs. While telling all this, the show card's message must be simple, factual, and informative.

Use the following guidelines for writing successful show card copy: (1) tell about the merchandise from the customer's viewpoint, (2) give the customer reasons to buy, (3) make the copy clear and interesting, (4) be believable, and (5) be brief.

How to Fit Copy Into Proper Formats:

1. The Lead-in Line — Why Buy? The customer will not buy without a reason. What will the merchandise do for the customer? Will it make life easier, give comfort, offer convenience, solve a problem, teach, entertain, flatter? Ask yourself this question for the lead-in line: "Why should the customer buy this merchandise?"

2. The Headline — What Are You Selling? The headline usually is used to identify merchandise. If the item is easily identified, the headline may be used to give a reason to buy or an important feature of the product. Example: "Wash and Wear."

3. The Body Copy — Give the Facts: Briefly tell features of the merchandise not obvious to the customer. Explain the quality, utility, ease of care, fabric content, fashion, value, selection, etc.

4. The Price — The Clincher: The price line helps close the sale. Price, in combination with the correct blend of other information on the show card, can give that final reason to buy. Make sure the price is correct. Do not use multiple pricing on show cards, except where "as advertised" or promotional items are involved.

This project will provide you with experience in developing copy that sells. You also will have an opportunity to make professional-size, hand-lettered show cards, using your own copy.

Select three newspaper advertisements. Following the previous suggestions for developing good copy, prepare the show card copy you would use in an interior display for each of the advertisements you have selected. Write that copy in the spaces provided and attach the three newspaper advertisements to this page with a paper clip.

Interior Display — Show Card Copy #1

Interior Display — Show Card Copy #2

Interior Display — Show Card Copy #3

After mastering the lettering skills that you will learn in Project 23, you will be ready to letter show cards, using the copy you prepared above. To assist in the layout, obtain three professionally made signs 11 inches wide by 14 inches long. Use these signs as guides in completing this assignment. Letter your signs on white paper or poster board cut to the appropriate size.

SECTION 4

PROJECT 23

Name _____

Course _____

Date Assigned _____

Estimated Finish _____

Date Finished _____

Evaluation _____

DEVELOPING SHOW CARD LETTERING SKILLS

Materials for interior display presentations usually are purchased from suppliers of display equipment. Point-of-purchase aids are generally available from manufacturers or suppliers. However, the display person still must prepare many items "on the spot" in order to have effective displays. The most frequently needed item of this type is the show card.

In the preparation of a show card, an idea is developed and a selling message devised. Next, the layout is roughed, using the display elements and principles that you already have learned. Then colors are selected, illustrations are chosen, and the show card is lettered and put into use. Some firms have a show card machine which is used in making signs. Other firms do not have such machines and prepare their show cards with hand lettering. Even in firms with machines, display workers frequently will letter by hand when only a few show cards are needed or when a show card is to be made for a special purpose. The ability to make neat, effective show cards is something display people can achieve with practice. With good tools and the patience to follow a few guidelines, you can produce attractive show cards.

The intent of this special project is to provide the display person with basic skills for constructing a highly readable uppercase alphabet (capitals), using the Coit pen. If Coit pens are not on hand, one-stroke show card lettering brushes, or wedge-shaped felt or nylon-tipped pens may be substituted. Directions purposely have been kept to a minimum. Once the display person has become oriented to the following system, the construction of letters, punctuation, and numbers will be accomplished with increasing ease.

1. Use white unwaxed wrapping paper for practice purposes.

2. A ⅜-inch Coit pen is appropriate for developing skills, although a wide range of pen sizes is available for various needs.

3. Use a 2½-inch vertical space within which to letter. It would be wise to cut a 2½-inch wide guideline stick (posterboard or hardboard) for purposes of rapidly ruling practice paper.

4. Black India ink is most effective for practice. Quality tempera paints in a wide range of colors can be used later when show cards, banners, and promotional materials are made.

5. In most cases, letter strokes are made from top to bottom and left to right.

6. The pen should be held like a pencil, but with the point at a 45-degree angle to the top and bottom guidelines.

7. Pressure should be put on the pen point to give added control in stroke construction.

8. The letters in this particular alphabet should be approximately 1½ inches wide.

1. Be sure to hold your pen at a 45-degree angle to the guidelines.

2. Keep the pen in full contact with the paper and do not hesitate to use moderate pressure.

3. PULL, do not push the pen.

4. Use the entire arm, not just the hand.

5. Watch the slant of the "I." It should move slighly from left to right.

6. Pause momentarily at the end of the stroke before lifting the pen straight up off the paper.

This is a basic stroke and should be perfected before you go on.

1. In making the first stroke (the crossbar of the "T"), hold the pen at the same angle as for the letter "I."

2. Make the stroke, using the entire arm, in one continuous motion. Make the crossbar touch the upper guideline all the way across (approximately 1½ inches).

3. The second stroke is like the letter "I."

Continue to watch the slant of the letter and the 45-degree angle of your pen.

1. First draw the letter "I." Then make a stroke like the cross stroke of "T," but placed at the bottom (about 1½-inches).

2. The entire letter is completed without lifting the pen from the paper.

1. The first stroke is the same as that for the "I."

2. The second stroke is like that of the top of the "T." Continue to maintain the 45-degree angle on the pen.

3. The third stroke is the same length as the second and is placed just below the midway point of the down stroke.

Always remember to work from left to right and from top to bottom.

1. The letter "E" is similar to the "F."

2. After drawing an "L," complete the "E" in the same manner as the "F."

Remember to keep constant pressure on your pen so that the flow of ink will be uniform.

1. The "H" is made by first drawing two parallel down strokes like the "I."

2. The third stroke, which joins the two parallel lines, should be placed just below the midpoint.

1. The first stroke is again the letter "I."

   Note: Lettering sequence is based on progressive steps.

2. Making the second stroke is like drawing an upside down and backwards "L," starting at the top of the first stroke, without lifting the pen.

3. The third stroke is the same as the crossbar used in the letter "H."

   Continue to check the 45-degree angle of the pen by observing consistency in stroke endings.

1. Two parallel down strokes are drawn, as in the "H."

2. The third stroke connects the top of the first stroke with the bottom of the second stroke.

3. Be sure that there is a 45-degree angle at the bottom of the third stroke.

   Check periodically to see that your lettering is slanting slightly from top left to bottom right.

1. The "M" will be wider than all previous letters because of the four-stroke construction.

2. The first two strokes are parallel down strokes.

3. The third stroke is similar to the third stroke of the "N" except that this stroke ends slightly

past the halfway point between the two vertical lines.

4. The fourth stroke starts at the top of the second stroke and crosses into the third stroke just above the bottom guideline. Note that this stroke violates the left-to-right rule.

1. The "V" is simply made of the third and fourth strokes of the "M."

2. Watch the ending angle (45 degrees) where the two strokes are joined.

1. The "W" is made by drawing two "V's" that are connected at the top in the middle. Like the "M," this letter is wider than most letters because of the four strokes used.

2. Be sure that all the angles where lines are joined are 45 degrees.

1. This letter is made wider at the bottom (1½ inches) than at the top in order to prevent the appearance of instability.

2. The first stroke is a diagonal drawn left to right, top to bottom.

3. The second stroke is a diagonal drawn right to left and top to bottom. Note that the second stroke, like stroke four of the "M," violates the left-to-right rule.

1. The first stroke is similar to the "X," but ends at the midpoint of the guidelines.

2. The second stroke begins at the upper guideline, meets the first stroke, and then continues straight down to the bottom guideline.

1. The first stroke is the letter "I."

2. The second stroke is like the second stroke of the letter "Y," but is is pulled down to the

right to complete the letter.

3. The width of the "K" at the base is greater than the width at the top.

1. The "Z" is made in one continuous stroke.

2. The top of the letter is made like the top of a "T." The stroke then is continued by PULLING the pen at the 45-degree angle down to the bottom line.

3. The letter is finished by repeating the top stroke of the letter, but along the bottom guideline.

4. The base of the "Z" should be slightly to the right of the top to prevent the appearance of tipping.

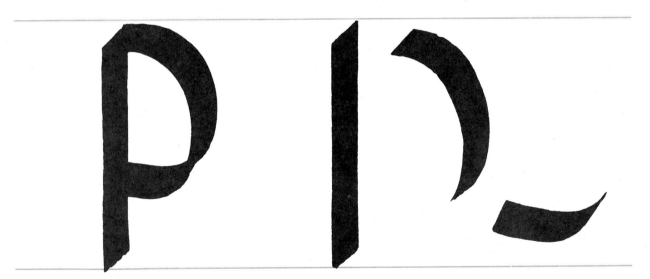

1. Again, the first stroke is the "I."

2. The second stroke starts at the top of the first stroke and is slowly pulled down in the shape of a half-moon to a point just below the middle of the space between guidelines.

3. The third stroke starts just below the mid-point of the "I" and is drawn across the paper into the second stroke.

4. Note the 45-degree angle where the second and third strokes join.

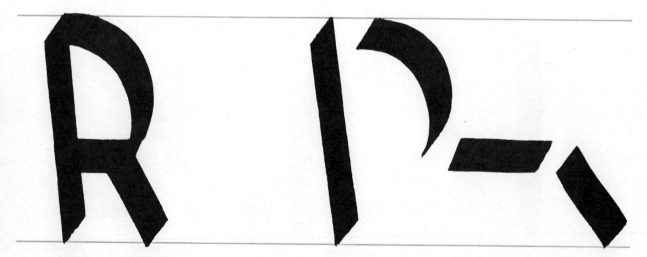

1. The first two strokes are like the first two strokes of the letter "P."

2. The third stroke is similar to the second stroke in the "P," and is pulled down into another half-moon which just touches the bottom guideline.

3. The fourth stroke is like the third stroke of the "P," joining the bottom of the "I" with stroke three.

   Again note 45-degree angles to test consistency in letter construction.

1. The first three strokes are the same as those used for the letter "P."

2. The fourth stroke is a short diagonal beginning just to the left of the intersection of the second and third strokes. It is pulled down to the right to complete the letter.

1. The first stroke is the letter "I."

2. The second stroke is a large half-moon drawn from the top of the "I" and pulled down to touch the bottom guideline.

3. The third stroke is pulled along the bottom guideline, left to right from the "I," and slipped into the second stroke.

1. The first stroke is started slightly below the top guideline and is pulled down and slightly to the left at first, then straight down until the base is reached.

2. Without lifting the pen, construct the base by pulling the pen sideways in a looping action and sliding the pen slightly upward. The base takes on the appearance of a rocking chair.

3. The second stroke places a small half-moon on the top of the "C."

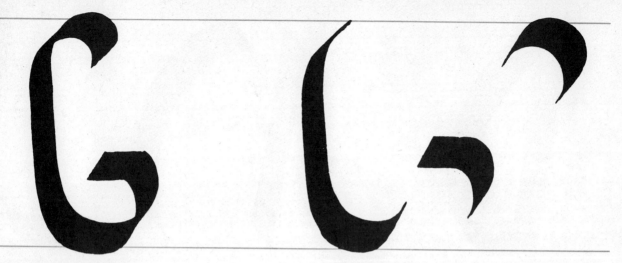

1. The first stroke is like that of the letter "C."

2. The second stroke starts slightly below the midpoint of the guidelines. It is pulled to the right and down to the left, into the end of the first stroke. Note the corner effect in the second stroke.

3. The third stroke is the same as the second stroke in the letter "C."

1. The first stroke is like that of the letter "C."

2. The second stroke is the first stroke in an upside down and reversed position.

3. Note the 45-degree angle where the two strokes are joined at the top and bottom.

4. This letter is not round, but instead has two flat sides and a slightly rounded base and top.

1. The first two strokes are the same as for the letter "O."

2. The third stroke is a short diagonal starting in the middle of the base of the "O" and continuing below the guideline.

1. The first stroke of the "U" starts like the "I" but is completed in a fashion similar to the first stroke of the "O."

2. The second stroke is like the "I" but slides left into the first stroke at the base.

1. The first stroke is similar to the base of the first stroke in the "U."

2. The second stroke repeats the second stroke of the "U."

1. The first stroke starts at the top of the paper, is curved downwards, then to the right, and then slightly to the left.

2. The second stroke completes the bottom loop, starting a third of the way up the paper and curving to the right and into the first stroke.

3. The third stroke is like the second stroke of the "C."

1. The first stroke is like the beginning of the first stroke of the letter "S."

2. The second stroke starts at the top, touching the first stroke, curving along the top, down

to the left, then back to the right to the bottom of the space, ending on a point.

3. The third stroke is the period.

1. The first stroke starts slightly above the guidelines and slants to the left.

2. The second stroke is accomplished with a slight break and continuation of the initial stroke.

1. Quotation marks are short, curved strokes and are placed about one third of the way down in the space. They are enlarged here to show the strokes.

1. The hyphen is made with one short stroke, slightly below the midpoint of the space.

2. The comma is one quotation mark, started slightly above the bottom guideline.

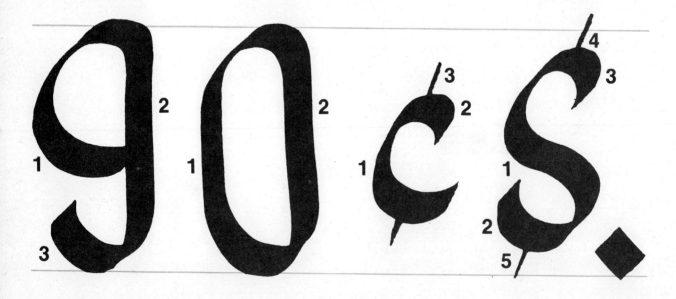

SECTION 5

PROJECT 24

Name ———————————————

Course ———————————————

Date Assigned ———————————————

Estimated Finish ———————————————

Date Finished ———————————————

Evaluation ———————————————

RECOGNIZING POINT-OF-PURCHASE DISPLAYS

In order to utilize point-of-purchase display materials effectively, retailers should be able to recognize quickly the various point-of-purchase units used in retail stores. There are ten common kinds of display units. Each is designed to serve a particular merchandising function. Those functions include advertising, selling, merchandising, and incentive program and promotion. Section 5 contains a description of each type of display unit and the functions it serves. This project provides experience in recognizing various types of point-of-purchase displays and in measuring their effectiveness. Visit several local stores and observe the location and use of an example of each type of point-of-purchase displays. Record your observations and evaluations in the spaces provided below and on the following page.

Point-of-Purchase Display	Name of Store	Location in Store	Product(s) Displayed	Merchandising Function
1. Counter Unit				
2. Sales Register Unit				
3. Floorstand Unit				
4. Freestanding Pole Unit				
5. Shelf Unit				
6. Tester Unit				
7. Wall Unit				
8. Full-Line Merchandiser Unit				
9. Incentive and Premium Unit				
10. Sign Unit				

Evaluate the point-of-purchase displays you identified on the previous page. Use a scale of 1-10, with 1 being the lowest possible score and 10 the highest. Give reasons for your rating and indicate how you would improve each display.

1. Counter Unit: Rating _____

Reasons _____

Suggestions for improvement _____

2. Sales Register Unit: Rating _____

Reasons _____

Suggestions for improvement _____

3. Floorstand Unit: Rating _____

Reasons _____

Suggestions for improvement _____

4. Freestanding Pole Unit: Rating _____

Reasons _____

Suggestions for improvement _____

5. Shelf Unit: Rating _____

Reasons _____

Suggestions for improvement _____

6. Tester Unit: Rating _____

Reasons _____

Suggestions for improvement _____

7. Wall Unit: Rating _____

Reasons _____

Suggestions for improvement _____

8. Full-Line Merchandiser Unit: Rating _____

Reasons _____

Suggestions for improvement _____

9. Incentive and Premium Unit: Rating _____

Reasons _____

Suggestions for improvement _____

10. Sign Unit: Rating _____

Reasons _____

Suggestions for improvement _____

SECTION 5

PROJECT 25

Name _____

Estimated Finish _____

Course _____

Date Finished _____

Date Assigned _____

Evaluation _____

LOCATING AND PLACING POINT-OF-PURCHASE DISPLAYS

In most cases, point-of-purchase display materials are designed and produced by display manufacturers. Suggestions for locating displays in a retail store often are provided by the distributors of the product being promoted. Retailers, however, usually make the final decision as to where a particular point-of-purchase unit will be placed.

This project asks you to (1) identify the placement of at least five point-of-purchase displays in a store of your choice, (2) draw a rough sketch of the store's layout and show (by numbering) where each display currently is located, (3) indicate any changes you would make in the location of the displays, and (4) give reasons for your suggested changes.

Original Store Layout (Sketch)

Suggested Store Layout (Sketch)

Reasons for change:

Display Number

Reasons

_____   _____

_____   _____

_____   _____

_____   _____

Provide a rough sketch of a retail store of your choice. Using the ten kinds of point-of-purchase display units, (1) show (by number) where you would locate each display, and (2) indicate the kind of merchandise you would use in each unit. Be prepared to discuss your decisions.

Point-of-Purchase Display Units

Number of Display Unit

1. Counter Unit
2. Sales Register Unit
3. Floorstand Unit
4. Freestanding Pole Unit
5. Shelf Unit

6. Tester Unit
7. Wall Unit
8. Full-Line Merchandiser Unit
9. Incentive and Premium Unit
10. Sign Unit

Store Sketch

Kinds of Merchandise

Number of Display Unit

1. _____
2. _____
3. _____
4. _____
5. _____

6. _____
7. _____
8. _____
9. _____
10. _____

SECTION 5

PROJECT 26

Name _____

Course _____

Date Assigned _____

Estimated Finish _____

Date Finished _____

Evaluation _____

POINT-OF-PURCHASE SYSTEMS AND SOURCES

In order to organize better the rapidly growing number of products sold to the public, merchants are making greater use of display units that will departmentalize or compartmentalize merchandise. Four basic point-of-purchase display designs have been created to help the merchant organize merchandise. These systems are (1) the shelf management system, (2) the frame-out system, (3) the air space system, and (4) the boutique system. Section 5 includes a description of each type of system. This project provides an opportunity to view and evaluate the effectiveness of each type of system. This project also asks you to identify sources for point-of-purchase displays.

Locate four retail stores, each of which uses a different one of the point-of-purchase systems mentioned above. Provide the needed information in the appropriate spaces below.

1. Store Name _____

   Point-of-Purchase System _____

   System Advantages _____

   System Disadvantages _____

2. Store Name _____

   Point-of-Purchase System _____

   System Advantages _____

   System Disadvantages _____

3. Store Name _____

   Point-of-Purchase System _____

   System Advantages _____

   System Disadvantages _____

4. Store Name _____

   Point-of-Purchase System _____

   System Advantages _____

   System Disadvantages _____

Sources of Point-of-Purchase Displays

Select three different retail stores in your area. Ask each merchant to respond to the questions listed below. Compare the answers you receive and be prepared to discuss the results.

Store Number 1

Type of Store _____

Where POP material is obtained _____

Purchased or free? _____

Prepackaged or units only? _____

Who selects locations? _____

Other observations _____

_____

Store Number 2

Type of Store _____

Where POP material is obtained _____

Purchased or free? _____

Prepackaged or units only? _____

Who selects locations? _____

Other observations _____

_____

Store Number 3

Type of Store _____

Where POP material is obtained _____

Purchased or free? _____

Prepackaged or units only? _____

Who selects locations? _____

Other observations _____

_____

SECTION 5

PROJECT 27

Name _____

Estimated Finish _____

Course _____

Date Finished _____

Date Assigned _____

Evaluation _____

NEW USES FOR POINT-OF-PURCHASE DISPLAYS

After a period of time, some point-of-purchase displays may be altered (with the approval of the suppliers) for different uses or to be made more effective. For example, a point-of-purchase display function may be changed from advertising to selling, merchandising, or incentive-promotion. It also may be possible to rearrange merchandise in a display by adding or removing a shelf or platform. Even the appearance of the display might be changed by framing in or redoing the display's surface. Such changes can be effective if the display person uses creativity and understands the principles and elements of display.

Select a point-of-purchase display in a local store that you feel could be put to a different use. Provide a brief description of the display and describe how you would enhance or change its use to make it more effective. (If possible, try to obtain an actual display unit and make the changes suggested in your plan.)

Type of Display _____

_____

Original Function _____

_____

Function of Altered Display _____

_____

Theme of Display _____

_____

Description of Intended Changes _____

_____

_____

_____

_____

_____

_____

Utilizing the information you provided on the previous page, sketch your proposed changes in the space below.

New Point-of-Purchase Display Sketch

Make a list of the materials and tools you will need to complete the display project.

Materials needed _____

_____

_____

Tools needed _____

_____

_____

SECTION 5

PROJECT 28

Name _____

Estimated Finish _____

Course _____

Date Finished _____

Date Assigned _____

Evaluation _____

EVALUATING POINT-OF-PURCHASE DISPLAYS

Evaluate the effectiveness of the changes you have made in the original point-of-purchase display unit, using the rating scale provided below. Rate each factor by checking a point somewhere on the scale. Checking "1" would indicate that you feel the display is weak on that particular factor. Checking "10" would indicate that the display is extremely strong on that factor. Provide comments to support your evaluation.

Power to Attract Attention

0 1 2 3 4 5 6 7 8 9 10

Comments _____

_____

_____

Arrangement

0 1 2 3 4 5 6 7 8 9 10

Comments _____

_____

_____

Function Clearly Identified

0 1 2 3 4 5 6 7 8 9 10

Comments _____

_____

_____

Timeliness

0 1 2 3 4 5 6 7 8 9 10

Comments _____

_____

_____

Appearance and Quality of Work

0 1 2 3 4 5 6 7 8 9 10

Comments _____

_____

_____

You should ask at least two other individuals to evaluate your work, using the rating scale on the previous page. Compare your evaluation and comments with those you obtain from these two people. Consider any final changes you should make. Sketch these changes in the space provided and identify any additional materials and tools needed to complete the task.

Point-of-Purchase Display Sketch (Changes)

Additional materials _____

Additional tools _____

Compare your original display sketch with the one shown above. Were any major changes made? Is the new display more effective than the original unit?

_____

_____

_____

_____

_____

SECTION 6

PROJECT 29

Name _____

Course _____

Date Assigned _____

Estimated Finish _____

Date Finished _____

Evaluation _____

ANALYSIS OF ADVERTISING DISPLAYS AND EXHIBITS

Exhibits and advertising displays are the main feature of many public fairs, trade shows, industrial expositions, professional conventions, and other settings that attract large numbers of potential buyers. Exhibits and advertising displays come in a great variety of sizes and designs and serve many purposes. In this project, you are asked to locate one advertising display and two exhibits in your community or in nearby cities. First be sure that the advertising display and the exhibits you are considering really fit those categories. Complete an analysis of each by answering the questions under each heading.

Advertising Display

Display Location: _____

Sponsor of Display: _____

Products Featured: _____

_____

Display Description: (How are the products presented?) _____

_____

_____

Viewers: (purchasing representatives, direct consumers, travelers, etc.) _____

_____

_____

Display Design: (construction, color, layout) _____

_____

_____

_____

Display Effectiveness: _____

_____

Exhibit One

Exhibit Location: _____

Sponsor of Exhibit: _____

Type of Exhibit: (permanent, transportable, single-event) _____

                    (staffed or unstaffed) _____

Products Featured: _____

Exhibit Description: (How are the products presented?) _____

_____

_____

_____

Clientele: _____

Exhibit Design: (construction, color, layout) _____

_____

_____

_____

Exhibit Effectiveness: _____

_____

Exhibit Two

Exhibit Location: _____

Sponsor of Exhibit: _____

Type of Exhibit: (permanent, transportable, single-event) _____

                    (staffed or unstaffed) _____

Products Featured: _____

Exhibit Description: (How are the products presented?) _____

_____

_____

_____

Clientele: _____

Exhibit Design: (construction, color, layout) _____

_____

_____

_____

Exhibit Effectiveness: _____

_____

SECTION 6

PROJECT 30

Name _____

Course _____

Date Assigned _____

Estimated Finish _____

Date Finished _____

Evaluation _____

DECIDING WHETHER TO EXHIBIT

Exhibits, like other forms of visual presentation, are intended to present and sell products to potential customers. A major decision that many firms must make is whether they should prepare and present an exhibit. In Section 6 of this text, a number of questions are listed that must be considered in making a decision about exhibiting.

In this project, you are given three case situations. After reading each case, decide whether or not the firm should prepare and present an exhibit, given the circumstances described. Be sure to justify your decision with supporting statements or explanations. Use additional sheets of paper for your answers if necessary.

Springtown Manufacturing Company

Springtown Manufacturing Company produces metal fabricated office furniture and factory benches and it recently has added a line of metal home and outdoor furniture. The company is planning to expand its main plant by 45,000 square feet, allowing an increase of 15 to 20 percent in production capacity. Springtown has developed a large number of customers, mostly wholesalers, in all parts of the country.

Within the metal fabricating industry there are several annual trade shows that attract a large number of customers for the types of items produced by Springtown Manufacturing. The company has not exhibited at these or any other shows. It has sent representatives to the shows to make personal contact with current and potential customers. Several competitors have exhibited regularly at these shows. The marketing manager for Springtown Manufacturing feels that the firm should develop an exhibit that could be presented at several of the trade shows.

1. What advantages and disadvantages would there be to Springtown Manufacturing exhibiting at the

    metal fabricating trade shows? _____

    _____

    _____

2. Should Springtown Manufacturing prepare and present an exhibit at these shows? Explain fully the

    reasons for your decision. _____

    _____

    _____

    _____

    _____

Prairie Foods Incorporated

Prairie Foods Incorporated is a locally owned company that operates a sunflower seed gathering plant. The plant has a storage capacity of nearly 300,000 bushels. In addition, it serves as a collector and storage facility for other specialty crops, such as mustard. The owner of the firm plans to open a second plant about 100 miles from the present location in order to serve a larger area. Prairie Foods Inc. buys from local producers and then resells in larger quantities to processors located around the country. The owner of Prairie Foods has been contacted by a representative of a farm products exhibition center. The exhibition center would like Prairie Foods to set up a permanent display at the center. People coming to the exhibition center are mostly tourists and travelers. Prairie Foods Inc. does not sell to ultimate consumers or prepare any consumer food products.

1. Should Prairie Foods prepare and present an exhibit at the exhibition center? _____

    _____

2. Explain fully the reasons for your decision. _____

    _____

    _____

    _____

    _____

Sunshine Fashions

Sunshine Fashions is a clothing design and manufacturing company which sells direct to retail stores. It provides a complete line of women's ready-to-wear sports clothing for ages 12 and older. Over the past 26 years, Sunshine Fashions has grown from a local west coast manufacturing firm to a nationally known company with distribution to stores in all states. Each representative of Sunshine Fashions attends at least two of the regional clothing shows each year. At these shows representatives present their new lines of sportswear. Almost all of the people attending the shows are owners or buyers from women's specialty stores or departments. Sunshine Fashions' first contact with new customers is usually through these shows. Sales made at the shows account for nearly 40 percent of Sunshine Fashions' annual business. Because the shows take up a great deal of time for at least four of the company's executives, the question is being raised as to whether the firm should continue to exhibit at these shows.

1. Should Sunshine Fashions continue to exhibit at regional clothing shows? _____

    _____

2. Explain fully the reasons for your decision. _____

    _____

    _____

    _____

SECTION 6

PROJECT 31

Name _____

Course _____

Date Assigned _____

Estimated Finish _____

Date Finished _____

Evaluation _____

DESIGN OF A PERMANENT EXHIBIT

Display workers sometimes are asked to design and construct exhibits for use by business firms. Given a certain amount of information, the display worker is expected to apply skill and creativity to the preparation of an appropriate exhibit. In this project, you are to study the request by Quality Brick and Tile Company. Then, on the reverse side of this sheet, sketch and explain the exhibit you would recommend.

Exhibit Request

Company: Quality Brick and Tile Company
Magnolia Road

Products: All types of building brick, fire brick, cement blocks, clay tile, and precast cement units such as steps and culverts. Material comes in standard sizes and designs as well as in decorative and special designs.

Main Features: High quality; precise dimensions; wide variety of materials; prompt delivery direct from factory to building site.

Clientele: Residential and commercial building contractors, retail home-building supply firms, and, to a limited extent, buyers of commercial and residential buildings.

Exhibit Location: Regional airport lobby.

Exhibit Description: Permanent type to be located in lobby area of regional airport. Size can vary from four to six feet square, open on all four sides. Exhibit to be floor-mounted with electrical service accessed through pedestal of exhibit. Since it will not be staffed, the exhibit should be designed with a brochure rack.

Requirements: The regional airport permits special lighting effects from the ceiling only. The exhibit and floor surface around it must be kept free of obstructions and surfaces that might be dangerous to viewers. The regional airport lobby contains 36 exhibits by national, state, and local firms. Exhibits must be installed for a minimum of one year.

Sketch of Exhibit

Sketch in the space below the exhibit you recommend for Quality Brick and Tile Company.

_____

_____

Describe the materials and colors you recommend in this exhibit. _____

_____

_____

_____

Give the reasons why you recommend this particular exhibit for the Quality Brick and Tile Company.

_____

_____

_____

_____

_____

_____

SECTION 6

PROJECT 32

Name _____

Course _____

Date Assigned _____

Estimated Finish _____

Date Finished _____

Evaluation _____

DESIGN OF A PORTABLE EXHIBIT

The West Lawn Business Association is made up of 31 retail firms. Through the Association, the firms attempt to carry out a wide variety of efforts to promote their businesses, all located in the West Lawn shopping area. The businesses include two department stores, one boutique, one variety store, three shoe stores, one fabric store, one bank, two supermarkets, one drug store, two hardware stores, one sporting-goods store, one book and card shop, one office equipment and fast-copy store, one insurance office, two beverage stores, two restaurants, two automotive service stations, one bakery, one ice-cream store, two women's specialty stores, one men's specialty store, and one jewelry store. Promotional efforts by the West Lawn Business Association frequently include free gifts to customers from member merchants, sponsorship of softball and bowling teams, demonstrations by artists and craft specialists, children's movies, and seasonal programs of music, displays, and plays.

In the area served by the West Lawn businesses, there are several annual shows such as sports shows, county fairs, farm and home expositions, and horse and pet shows. The West Lawn Business Association would like a portable unstaffed exhibit that could be set up at these shows. The exhibit should emphasize the convenience of the West Lawn shopping area, the excellent businesses, the good parking, and the community spirit of the West Lawn Business Association.

The exhibit should be no larger than 4 feet wide, 8 feet long, and 8 feet high. When collapsed for transportation or storage, it should fit into three containers of a size and weight that could be lifted by two persons and carried in a regular-size station wagon.

In the space below, describe what theme, ideas, or products should be featured in the exhibit. On the reverse side of this sheet, draw a sketch of the exhibit you would recommend. Describe fully the materials you would use in the construction of the exhibit.

Information to Be Featured

_____

_____

_____

_____

_____

_____

_____

_____

Sketch of Exhibit

Draw a rough sketch of the exhibit you recommend for the West Lawn Business Association.

_____

_____

Explanation of Construction

Describe the materials to be used in construction of the exhibit, and note recommended colors and lighting.

_____

_____

_____

_____

_____

_____

_____

_____

_____

SECTION 6

PROJECT 33

Name _____	Estimated Finish _____
Course _____	Date Finished _____
Date Assigned _____	Evaluation _____

GUIDELINES FOR EVALUATING DISPLAYS AND EXHIBITS

Advertising displays and exhibits, like retail store displays, should be given a careful check before being opened for public view. The usual features of any display should be considered, and any additional or different features peculiar to exhibits also must be considered. In this project, you are to develop a checklist that could be used to make sure that an exhibit or an advertising display is ready for public viewing. On the sample form below, seven items are suggested. Add other items, so that you have an all-inclusive list that can be used for a variety of exhibits and displays. Some items may not apply to every display or exhibit. Continue this form on additional sheets of paper as needed.

Item	Condition of Item			Does Not Apply to This Display
	Excellent	Satisfactory	Needs Attention	
Backdrop or background				
Tables or props				
Business identification (logo)				
Lights and lighting				
Electrical cords and connections				
Products				
Literature				

In this part of Project 33, you will test your checklist on two different exhibits. Make two copies of your checklist, then evaluate two exhibits in your community. (If exhibits are not available in your community, check with your instructor on the use of pictures of exhibits.) In the spaces below, describe how well your checklist worked for each exhibit and make recommendations for changes in the checklist and in the exhibit.

Exhibit One

Business: _____ **Location:** _____

Products Featured: _____

_____

List any items you had to add to your checklist: _____

_____

What features of this exhibit need attention? _____

_____

What should be done to improve this exhibit? _____

_____

_____

_____

Exhibit Two

Business: _____ **Location:** _____

Products Featured: _____

List any items you had to add to your checklist: _____

_____

What features of this exhibit need attention? _____

_____

What should be done to improve this exhibit? _____

_____

_____

_____

SECTION 7

PROJECT 34

Name _____

Course _____

Date Assigned _____

Estimated Finish _____

Date Finished _____

Evaluation _____

DEVELOPING CREATIVE DISPLAY IDEAS

Effective displays usually result when the display person has a clear idea of what the finished display should look like. There are many sources for creative display ideas. Utilizing these sources can save time and effort and produce displays that will sell merchandise. Some excellent sources for ideas include the merchandise itself, publications, the displays of other merchants, customers, store promotions, and personal display files. Very often the experienced display designer will combine several ideas from these sources to construct a single display. This project provides opportunities for you to become acquainted with various display resources and to practice developing creative display ideas.

Merchandise

For each item of merchandise below, list some customer uses and briefly describe an idea you would use to build a display for that merchandise.

Item	Customer Uses	Creative Display Idea
Weight-lifting Equipment		
Portable T.V.		
Ten-Speed Bike		
Waterproof Jacket		
Jogging Shoes		

Printed Material

Select an item of merchandise for which you would like to design a display. Complete the following steps and record the results on a separate piece of paper.

✔ Check off number upon completion.

___1. Gather all available trade publications, newspapers, magazines, or other media which might contain pictures of or advertisements for the product you have selected.

___2. Obtain permission, where necessary, to remove the information from the publications you have collected.

___3. Identify and photocopy or cut out at least three different examples of advertisements or pictures displaying your product.

___4. On a separate sheet of paper, explain how you would combine the display ideas contained in the advertisements or pictures into a single merchandise display. Attach these materials to your paper.

Displays of Other Merchants

Select one item of merchandise currently being displayed in local retail stores. Complete the following steps and record the results on a separate piece of paper.

✔ Check off number upon completion.

___1. Locate three different in-store displays that present the merchandise you have selected.

___2. If possible, obtain permission to photograph each display. If camera equipment is not available, roughly sketch each display so that obvious differences among the three displays can be seen.

___3. On a separate sheet of paper, explain how you would combine the display ideas contained in the photographs or sketches into a single merchandise display. Attach the photographs or sketches to your paper.

Customer Opinions

Use the following questions to obtain customer opinions about particular displays. There are separate lists of questions for customers in the store and customers who are leaving the store.

✔   Check off number upon completion.

____1. After obtaining the store management's approval, record the opinions of ten customers in the store and ten customers leaving the store. Use appropriate questions from the list below.

____2. Summarize the results of each set of questions and your personal reactions to the customers' answers on a separate piece of paper.

In-Store Questions

1. Are you a regular customer of this store?

2. What is your opinion of this particular display? (Select a display in advance.)

3. What do you like about this display? What do you dislike?

4. If you needed the displayed product, would you buy it because of the way it is presented here?

5. What is your favorite type of display? Why is that type your favorite?

Out-of-Store Questions

1. Are you a regular customer of this store?

2. Was there one particular display in the store that caught your attention?

3. Why do you remember that display?

4. What kind of merchandise does it contain?

5. Where in the store is this display located?

6. Did you purchase the displayed merchandise?

7. Do you think that the display helped you make your choice?

8. What kinds of displays would you like to see used more often in retail stores?

9. Do you feel that merchandise displays play an important part in helping you to make buying decisions? How?

Store Promotions

For each of the store promotions mentioned below, (1) describe a display idea that you feel would be appropriate for that event, and (2) list the kind(s) of merchandise you feel would be appropriate for that store promotion and for your display idea.

Store Promotion	Display Idea	Merchandise Used
Back to School		
Spring Cleaning		
Surf and Sand		
Presidents' Day		
White Sale		

Personal Files

In order to begin your own personal file of display ideas, complete the following steps: (1) Find at least one example (picture or illustration) of each of the store promotions listed below. (2) Write the name of each store promotion on a large envelope. Place the appropriate pictures or illustrations in the envelopes for future use.

This is an easy way to start a personal file of display ideas. You will want to collect and file additional display ideas as you encounter them.

New Year's Day	Memorial Day	Vacation
Lincoln's Birthday	May Day	Labor Day
Valentine's Day	Mother's Day	School Opening
Washington's Birthday	Father's Day	Autumn
St. Patrick's Day	Flag Day	Columbus Day
First Day of Spring	First Day of Summer	Thanksgiving
Easter	Graduation	Veterans' Day
April Fools' Day	Independence Day	Christmas

SECTION 7

PROJECT 35

Name _____

Course _____

Date Assigned _____

Estimated Finish _____

Date Finished _____

Evaluation _____

CREATING VISUAL PRESENTATIONS

The purpose of display is to sell merchandise. Once the merchandise to be displayed has been selected, an idea of how best to present that merchandise must be created. In Project 34 you learned that display ideas may come from many sources. After a display idea has been developed, it may be described in a single phrase, referred to as the "theme" of the display. The theme must be clear, concise (no more than four or five words), creative, and attention-getting. Themes often are printed on show cards or window signs and placed in displays to make sure that customers quickly recognize the ideas being presented.

Below are examples of themes which have been used to describe actual display ideas. They have unlimited uses and could spark your imagination to create new display themes.

Display Themes

APPLIANCES AND ELECTRICAL HOUSEWARES

"Make a Clean Sweep"
"Cook Modern — Cook Electronically"

HARDWARE

"Every Hobby Starts Here"
"Make Repair Work Fun"

HOME FURNISHINGS

"Cheerful House"
"Let the Sun Shine In"
"Carpets Like Clouds"
"Fashion by the Houseful"

SPORTING GOODS

"High Scoring . . . ."
"A Game for All Seasons"
"Make a Dash for Fitness"

CHILDREN'S AND INFANTS' WEAR

"The Smock Set"
"Grand Gifts for Grandparents"
"Bundles of Joy"

FASHION JEWELRY

"Worth Its Weight in Gold"
"Ear-resistible Beauty"

VACATION

"To Sea and Be Seen"
"Out-of-Doorables"
"Fun in the Sun"
"Vacation with Play"

SHOES

"Fashion Footwear"
"News Afoot"

Observe displays in ten different businesses. Write the name of each business in the left-hand column below. Then indicate the theme of each display, whether the theme is printed on a sign, and the merchandise being displayed.

Name of Business	Theme of Display	Theme Printed?	Merchandise in Display
1.		—— yes —— no	
2.		—— yes —— no	
3.		—— yes —— no	
4.		—— yes —— no	
5.		—— yes —— no	
6.		—— yes —— no	
7.		—— yes —— no	
8.		—— yes —— no	
9.		—— yes —— no	
10.		—— yes —— no	

Merchandise to be displayed is given in the left-hand column below. For each kind of merchandise, indicate a display idea and a possible theme for the sign.

Display Merchandise	Display Idea	Possible Theme
Radial Tires		
Blue Jeans		
Telephones		
Dress Shoes		
Suitcases		
Raincoats		

The Tempo Clothing Store is located in a shopping center at a busy intersection in a city of 65,000 people. Potential customer traffic past the display windows is heavy. The store has just received an excellent stock of national-brand men's and women's blue jeans. These jeans will be offered for sale at 20 percent off the regular retail price. The store management would like a jean display, with a strong sales appeal, in one of the windows.

Complete the planning sheet below. Then provide a rough sketch of your display design.

Merchandise for Display: _____

_____

_____

Display Idea: _____

_____

_____

_____

Display Theme for Sign: _____

_____

Window Sketch

Open display area 9 feet long, 6 feet high, 4 feet deep (no back)

Wilson Jewelry Store is one of 150 retail stores located in the North Shopping Center in a community of 750,000 residents. A special purchase of watches to be sold as gifts for spring graduates has arrived, and area graduation exercises are just a month away. The Wilsons would like a window display design featuring the watches as gifts.

Complete the planning sheet below. Then provide a rough sketch of your display design.

Merchandise for Display: _____

_____

_____

Display Idea: _____

_____

_____

_____

Display Theme for Sign: _____

_____

Window Sketch

Closed display area 9 feet long, 6 feet high, 2 feet deep

SECTION 7

PROJECT 36

Name _____

Course _____

Date Assigned _____

Estimated Finish _____

Date Finished _____

Evaluation _____

SKETCHING DISPLAY PRESENTATIONS

Drawing an idea on paper before constructing the display is essential to good planning. This drawing is a rough sketch of what will be in the display and how it will be arranged. Frequent practice soon will prove that a good idea can be communicated more quickly if you have a sketch to show. The display person does not have to be an accomplished artist. Remember, these are only rough sketches. Detailed drawings are not necessary and are not a good use of the display person's time. The sketch will serve its purpose if the display person just draws the shapes of objects and keeps them in proportion. (A pencil with soft, thick lead works best for sketching.)

In this project, you are to sketch three displays you have seen. At the bottom of each, indicate the elements and principles used in the display.

Display 1

What were the major display elements used in this display? _____

What major display principles were used? _____

Display 2

What were the major display elements used in this display? _____

What major display principles were used? _____

Display 3

What were the major display elements used in this display? _____

What major display principles were used? _____

SECTION 7

PROJECT 37

Name _____

Course _____

Date Assigned _____

Estimated Finish _____

Date Finished _____

Evaluation _____

PLANNING DISPLAY PRESENTATIONS

Planning is a major factor in the success of any retail business. Planning is of particular importance to people responsible for designing displays that will sell merchandise. Long-range display planning usually takes two forms: (1) the display-planning calendar, which is a listing of all displays to be built during the year, and (2) the display-planning budget, which is a record of expected costs involved in designing and constructing planned displays. This project provides you with opportunities to determine merchant attitudes toward the use of display-planning calendars and display-planning budgets.

Identify two retailers who use display-planning calendars in scheduling merchandise displays. Record each retailer's answers to the following questions:

Retailer 1 _____   **Retailer 2** _____

1. How far in advance do you plan your displays?

   Retailer 1 _____

   Retailer 2 _____

2. What are the advantages of a display-planning calendar?

   Retailer 1 _____

   Retailer 2 _____

3. Are there any disadvantages of a display-planning calendar?

   Retailer 1 _____

   Retailer 2 _____

4. Who is responsible for putting the display-planning calendar together?

   Retailer 1 _____

   Retailer 2 _____

5. What procedures are followed in completing the display-planning calendar?

   Retailer 1 _____

   Retailer 2 _____

Obtain from a retailer of your choice the information asked for in this display-planning calendar. Record the retailer's responses in the appropriate spaces.

Display-Planning Calendar		Store Name _____
Month	**Merchandise to Be Displayed**	**Display Idea/Theme**

Select a different retailer and obtain the display-planning budget information necessary to complete the form below. On the basis of the information you obtain, also answer the three questions below the form.

Display-Planning Budget		Store Name _____	
Month	**Merchandise to Be Used**	**Display Idea/Theme**	**Budget Cost to Display**

1. How far in advance do you budget for your displays? _____

2. How are individual display costs determined? _____

3. Can you change your budget once it is set up? _____

SECTION 8

PROJECT 38

Name _____

Estimated Finish _____

Course _____

Date Finished _____

Date Assigned _____

Evaluation _____

SOURCES OF VISUAL PRESENTATION MATERIALS

When you are planning and building a visual presentation, you need to know what materials are available in your display shop and from suppliers in your area. You may be planning a visual presentation to be used several months from now or you may be in the process of an installation. In either case, you will want some ready references to sources of certain materials. In this project, you are asked to develop a resource file of local suppliers of display materials. On the reverse side of this sheet you will find a form that can be used to record necessary information about a supplier. Before beginning, make several copies of the form, so that you will have one form for each supplier. On the form below, list at least two resources for each category of display material. By numbering each copy of the suppliers sheet and cross-referencing each with the list below, you will have a ready reference for display materials available in your community or city.

Type of Display Material	Resource (Firm Name)	Sheet # __
Mannequins		
Decorative Trimming		
Panels		
Paper Products		
Display Letters		
Risers and Stands		
Paints		
Motion Devices		

Suppliers for Visual Presentation Materials

Sheet Number _____

Firm name _____   Phone Number (_____) _____

Contact person _____   Title _____

Address _____

City _____   State _____   Zip _____

Description of materials available:

_____

_____

_____

_____

_____

_____

_____

_____

_____

_____

_____

_____

_____

Terms of sale and shipping or delivery service:

_____

_____

_____

_____

Record of quality and dependability of prior purchases:

_____

_____

_____

_____

SECTION 8

PROJECT 39

Name _____

Course _____

Date Assigned _____

Estimated Finish _____

Date Finished _____

Evaluation _____

CHARACTERISTICS OF DISPLAY MATERIALS

A knowledgeable display worker is familiar with a wide variety of materials used in the preparation and construction of visual presentations. This familiarity includes some knowledge of the best uses of the material as well as the good and poor features of the material. In this project, you will collect samples of commonly used display materials and examine them for good and poor features. (For example, hardboard panels can be sawed easily and have some rigidity, but they may be difficult to staple or tack things to.) When possible, you should obtain actual samples of the materials, but if they are not available, pictures of the materials may be used. In addition to your own examination of materials in each of the three categories, you may find it useful to talk with persons in display work and obtain their views on the uses and features of each material.

Paper Materials (Seamless Paper, Tubing, Corrugated, Crepe, Special)

Material 1 — Description: _____

_____

Best Use: _____

Good Features: _____

Poor Features: _____

Material 2 — Description: _____

_____

Best Use: _____

Good Features: _____

Poor Features: _____

Material 3 — Description: _____

_____

Best Use: _____

Good Features: _____

Poor Features: _____

Panel Materials (Plywood, Hardboard, Gypsum Board, Foam Core, Acrylic)

Material 1 — Description: _____

Best Use: _____

Good Features: _____

Poor Features: _____

Material 2 — Description: _____

Best Use: _____

Good Features: _____

Poor Features: _____

Material 3 — Description: _____

Best Use: _____

Good Features: _____

Poor Features: _____

Fabric Materials (Felt, Taffeta, Velvet, Burlap)

Material 1 — Description: _____

Best Use: _____

Good Features: _____

Poor Features: _____

Material 2 — Description: _____

Best Use: _____

Good Features: _____

Poor Features: _____

Material 3 — Description: _____

Best Use: _____

Good Features: _____

Poor Features: _____

SECTION 8

PROJECT 40

Name _____

Course _____

Date Assigned _____

Estimated Finish _____

Date Finished _____

Evaluation _____

EQUIPMENT FOR A DISPLAY SHOP

"Lee's", a small department store, was started 21 years ago as a neighborhood variety store. Over the years it has expanded and added various clothing lines. It recently has announced plans for another expansion. Up to the present time, sales employees have handled the minor display work. A free-lance display specialist has been employed periodically to prepare and install major displays. Now, with larger sales and the planned expansion, the owners feel they should have their own display staff on a full-time basis. The store now has a small room with a show card machine and a few hand tools but no other display shop equipment.

The owners of Lee's have asked you to recommend tools and equipment for their new display shop which will be included in the upcoming expansion. The owners are not sure how much they will be able to, or should, spend on display equipment and tools. They ask that you list the items you would recommend if only $600 were available. You are to make this list in the spaces below, using additional sheets of paper as necessary. On the reverse side, on a second list, show what additional items you would recommend that the owners purchase if another $1000 were available. List each item, give a brief description of it, and provide an estimated cost for it.

Recommended $600 List of Display Tools and Equipment

Item	Description	Estimated Cost

Recommended $1,000 List of Additional Display Tools and Equipment

Item	Description	Estimated Cost

SECTION 8

PROJECT 41

Name_____

Course_____

Date Assigned_____

Estimated Finish_____

Date Finished_____

Evaluation_____

LAYOUT OF A DISPLAY SHOP

In the building expansion planned by the owners of Lee's, a basement room, 20 feet by 48 feet (960 square feet) is planned for a display shop. This space includes a room 10 by 13 feet for a display office and another room of the same size for storage or other use. The remaining space, 20 feet by 35 feet, is a single large open room. On the reverse side of this sheet is a sketch of the rooms planned. Draw on the layout sketch an arrangement of equipment, tool area, and construction area. Assume that you have all the equipment you suggested in both the $600 and $1000 lists developed in Project 40. The show card machine also will be placed in the display shop. The present show card room and one other room of the same size (each 160 square feet) in the present store will be used for display storage.

In the space below, describe the inventory system you would use to keep track of the display props stored in the two 160-square-foot rooms. The present inventory of props includes the following: 32 full-form mannequins (14 female, 8 male, 10 children); 11 torso forms of various sizes; 12 heads; 300 various-sized sign holders; 6 nail kegs; 21 plastic cubes (2-foot and 3-foot sizes); 6 large boxes of miscellaneous seasonal items (Christmas, Easter, Labor Day, Thanksgiving); 3 sections of cedar fencing (4 feet by 6 feet); 10 foam core panels (4 feet by 8 feet); 34 various-sized chrome elevation units; 20 various-sized stairway display units; 4 winged horses; and 6 pieces of antique furniture.

Description of Inventory System

_____

_____

_____

_____

_____

_____

_____

_____

_____

_____

_____

_____

Recommended Layout of Display Shop

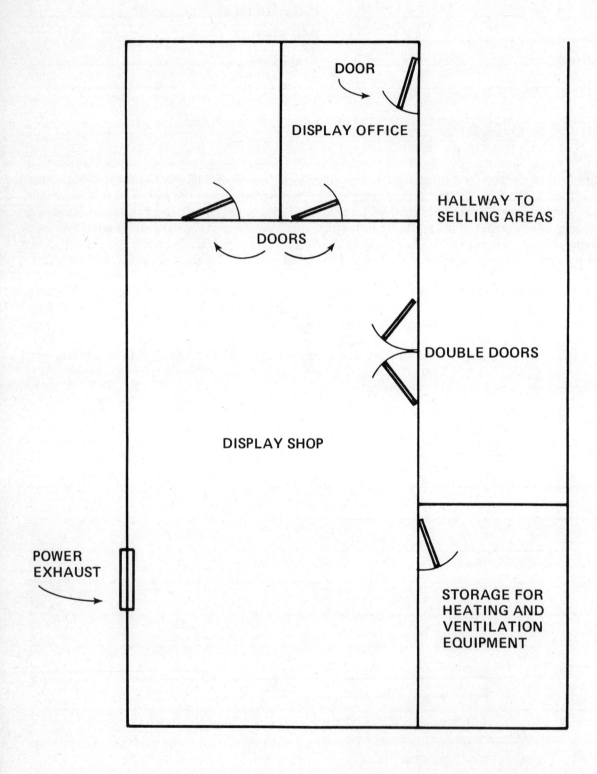

SECTION 8

PROJECT 42

Name _____

Estimated Finish _____

Course _____

Date Finished _____

Date Assigned _____

Evaluation _____

ESTIMATING COSTS

Below is a sketch of a display that the display director of a large department store would like to install in about six weeks. Because costs are always a concern for display workers, your director asks that you prepare a list of materials necessary for the display and estimate what it would cost for all materials except merchandise. Use the reverse side of this sheet to prepare your list and show your estimated costs. If you have questions about the materials or cost for any parts of the display, indicate your questions on the list or on a separate sheet of paper.

Overhead View

Dead tree — bleached gray

Clay pots — various sizes, light brown

Navajo-style rugs — three, with 6-inch back lift

Grass over entire floor

Front View

Backdrop — complete width and height, with sky, mountains, and sun

Cedar fence section

Merchandise:
   Western-cut jeans on fence
   Shirts on tree
   Boots on clay pots
   Belts and buckles on rugs

Item	Material	Estimated Cost

Total Estimated Material Cost _____

How many worker-hours would be required to prepare and install this display? _____

Explain how you arrived at the worker-hours needed. _____

_____

_____

_____

Using your local average hourly wage for display workers, what would be the labor cost for preparing and installing this display? _____   Total cost of materials and labor: _____ .

RECORD OF ASSIGNMENTS

Name _____   Course _____

Project	Dates		Instructor's Comments and Evaluation
	Assigned	Completed	
1			
2			
3			
4			
5			
6			
7			
8			
9			
10			
11			
12			
13			
14			
15			
16			
17			
18			
19			
20			
21			

RECORD OF ASSIGNMENTS

Name _____ Course _____

Project	Dates		Instructor's Comments and Evaluation
	Assigned	Completed	
22			
23			
24			
25			
26			
27			
28			
29			
30			
31			
32			
33			
34			
35			
36			
37			
38			
39			
40			
41			
42			

Index

Page numbers for definitions are in italics